Asian Words of Inspiration

Thoughts, motivational quotes and wisdom

from Asia's leading thinkers

on personal and professional success

and the journey of life.

By

Steven Howard

Asian Words of Inspiration

Asian Words of Inspiration

©2016 Steven Howard
All rights reserved.

No part of this Book may be reproduced or transmitted in any form or by any means, electronic or mechanical, including photocopying, recording, faxing, emailing, posting online or by any information storage and retrieval system, without written permission from the Author.

ISBN: 978-1-943702-08-4 (Print edition)
978-1-943702-09-1 (Kindle edition)

For reprint permission, please contact:
Steven Howard
c/o Caliente Press
1775 E Palm Canyon Drive, Suite 110-198
Palm Springs, CA 92264
U.S.A
Email: stevenhoward@verizon.net

Published by:
Caliente Press
1775 E Palm Canyon Drive, Suite 110-198
Palm Springs, CA 92264
U.S.A.
Email: CalientePress@verizon.net

Cover Design: Lee Chee Yih

Asian Words of Inspiration

Asian Words of Wisdom Series

The *Asian Words of Wisdom* series comprises the following titles:

Asian Words of Success — *Thoughts, quotations and phrases on leadership, marketing and personal development from Asia's leading thinkers.*

Asian Words of Meaning — *Reflections and thoughts on success, self-understanding and spiritual guidance from Asia's leading thinkers.*

Asian Words of Inspiration — *Thoughts, motivational quotes and wisdom from Asia's leading thinkers on personal and professional success and the journey of life.*

The Book of Asian Proverbs — *Unabridged collection of ancient sayings and teachings from across Asia.*

Indispensable Asian Words of Knowledge — *Words of wisdom from Asia's leading sages, philosophers, and statesmen. (October 2016)*

Asian Words of Inspiration

Asian Words of Inspiration

Dedication

This book is dedicated to

Zahida Rafaat Howard

Wonderful Mother. Good Friend. Loving Sister.

And an inspiration to many.

Asian Words of Inspiration

Asian Words of Inspiration

Table of Contents

Introduction	9
Self-Awareness	13
Mindfulness and Being Present	33
Peace and Peacefulness	61
Love	71
Your Life's Journey	85
Attaining Personal Goals	157
Interconnectedness	181
About the Author	193

Asian Words of Inspiration

Asian Words of Inspiration

Introduction

Quotations have long had the power to inspire. There is no innate, overwhelming feeling one can get like the one which arises from reading the words and thoughts of others and instinctively knowing how meaningful and applicable they are to one's own situation.

Words and thoughts are often the great seeds that lead to personal change. They are the building blocks that touch, provoke, arouse, and stir the individual passions and desires that stimulate personal inspiration and motivation.

Inspiration is different, however, from motivation. While motivation may get someone to do something or create something, inspiration produces sparks that set off new ideas, thoughts, and creativity.

Both may lead to action. Both may create purpose. Both may result in change. But in doing so they take different approaches.

The word inspiration comes from the Latin *inspirare*, which means "breathe into." By its very nature inspiration cannot be controlled or managed. However, it can be sparked, both consciously and unconsciously.

You can feed the unconscious aspect of inspiration as you allow the thoughts and quotations in *Asian Words of Inspiration* to percolate in your subconscious. You can also drive the conscious aspect of inspiration as you mentally apply these Asian words of wisdom to your life's journey.

Within *Asian Words of Inspiration* you will find over 700 motivational quotations, thoughts, and phrases from some of Asia's leading thinkers: Buddha, Confucius, Dalai Lama, Gandhi, Nisargadatta Maharaj, Lao-Tzu, Paramahansa Yogananda, Rumi and many others.

While we believe all of our sources for these quotations to be reliable, readers should not interpret *Asian Words of Inspiration* as a highly researched, authoritative reference book. This is not what we set out to do and it is certainly not what we have delivered.

What we have set out to do is gather and share the quotes that moved us, impressed us, or got us thinking a bit harder, deeper, or even more lightly. In achieving this endeavor, we trust you will agree, *Asian Words of Inspiration* does deliver.

Asian Words of Inspiration

While technically the continent of Asia extends all the way west to Turkey, most people today seem to cut Asia off at the western border of Pakistan. In truth, the boundaries of Asia are more culturally determined that geographic lines on maps and globes. As such, I have elected to include a handful of quotes from Persia (modern Iran), as well as notable people and cultures from the Middle East and Arabian Gulf regions.

These quotations will provide you with a wealth of beliefs and ideas to spark your own personal inspiration on: self-awareness, mindfulness and being present, peace and peacefulness, love, your life's journey, attaining personal goals, and the mystical, supernatural topic of interconnectedness.

May these *Asian Words of Inspiration* breathe new meaning, courage, and action into your life, resulting in both continued professional and personal success.

Steven Howard
August 2016

Asian Words of Inspiration

Asian Words of Inspiration

Self-Awareness

People with high levels of self-awareness have a clear and definite grasp of their own strengths and weaknesses. They also have a heightened ability to observe what motivates, de-motivates, satisfies, delights, troubles, and angers them.

Self-awareness is an on-going personal observation of what drives you to take the actions you take, to think the thoughts you think, and to feel the motions that bubble up inside you. This introspection needs to open, honest, and candid. Otherwise, you are only trying to fool yourself.

With a solid sense of self-awareness you multiply your predisposition to pursue the opportunities that are truly right for you. Likewise, you are also better positioned to prevent yourself from pursuing activities that are likely to have unsatisfying or potentially harmful results.

The journey of self-awareness is a long, and challenging one.

Hopefully the advice below from some of Asia's leading thinkers will help make your journey less difficult and more fruitful.

Asian Words of Inspiration

He who controls others may be powerful but he who has mastered himself is mightier still.

                                                         Lao-Tzu

The highest form of human intelligence is to observe yourself without judgment.

                                  Jiddu Krishnamurti

It is better to conquer yourself than to win a thousand battles.

                                                  Buddha

"Destroy evil" means to make the evil in your heart submit.

                                          Awa Kenzo

If you go on working with the light available, you will meet your Master, as he himself will be seeking you.

                                Sri Ramana Maharshi

If you think that you are bound, you remain bound; you make your own bondage. If you know that you are free, you are free this moment. This is knowledge, knowledge of freedom. Freedom is the goal of all nature.

                                Swami Vivekananda

Asian Words of Inspiration

The goal is the same for the one who meditates (on an object) and the one who practices self-inquiry. One attains stillness through meditation, the other through knowledge. One strives to attain something; the other seeks the one who strives to attain. The former takes a longer time, but in the end attains the Self.

Sri Ramana Maharshi

At any moment, you have a choice, that either leads you closer to your spirit or further away from it.

Thich Nhat Hanh

Find the seed at the bottom of your heart and bring forth a flower.

Shigenori Kameoka

The key to growth is the introduction of higher dimensions of consciousness into our awareness.

Lao-Tzu

Adversity is the foundation of virtue.

Japanese Proverb

What the gentleman seeks, he seeks within himself; what the small man seeks, he seeks in others.

Confucius

Asian Words of Inspiration

In order to pursue your goals with your whole heart, you must have a vision. In turn, your vision must be fueled by a deep seated belief that you will succeed. This means that sometimes you have to look beyond all the facts and go with your gut instinct. Unfortunately, other people will often view this act of courage, this act of faith in yourself, as unrealistic. I strongly disagree. As long as you believe in yourself and in your success, anything is possible. Don't wait for others to give you the go-ahead on your dreams. Trust yourself to succeed and you will.

Sri Ramana Maharshi
Absolute Consciousness

Sensations as such, however strong, do not cause suffering. It is the mind, bewildered by wrong ideas, addicted to thinking "I am this", "I am that", that fears loss and craves gain and suffers when frustrated.

Nisargadatta Maharaj

The superior man understands what is right; the inferior man understands what will sell.

Confucius

My objective is not to get rid of the ego, simply to be aware of how it leads me and where.

Deepak Chopra

Asian Words of Inspiration

Self-realized people do not see "others." The question of others does not arise. They will see one thing everywhere; the others are also included in that vision of the One. When you see the ocean, you have seen all the waters. There is no need of seeing different drops. The "other people" question will not arise, because they will be merged together with that Universal Being.

Swami Krishnananda Saraswati

He who experiences the unity of life sees his own Self in all beings, and all beings in his own Self, and looks on everything with an impartial eye.

Buddha

There are no conditions to fulfill. There is nothing to be done, nothing to be given up. Just look and remember, whatever you perceive is not you, nor yours. It is there in the field of consciousness, but you are not the field and its contents, nor even the knower of the field. It is your idea that you have to do things that entangles you in the results of your efforts — the motive, the desire, the failure to achieve, the sense of frustration — all this holds you back. Simply look at whatever happens and know that you are beyond it.

Nisargadatta Maharaj

Asian Words of Inspiration

To learn the Way we first kill off the chief hoodlum. What is the chief hoodlum? It is the emotions. We need to wipe out that den of thieves to see once again the clear, calm, wide open, original essence of mind. Don't let conditioned senses spy in. What is this about? It is about quelling the mind. One removes emotions to quell the mind, then purifies the mind to nurture its great elixir.

Ancestor Lu

Within everyone is an unlimited reservoir of energy, intelligence and happiness.

Maharishi Mahesh Yogi

The source of all creation is pure consciousness....pure potentiality seeking expression from the unmanifest to the manifest. And when we realize that our true Self is one of pure potentiality, we align with the power that manifests everything in the universe.

Deepak Chopra

Leave all worries behind and make your heart totally pure, like the face of a mirror with no image or design. Once your heart is cleansed of all images, it will contain them all.

Rumi

Asian Words of Inspiration

If we talk of knowing the Self, there must be two selves, one a knowing self, another the self which is known, and the process of knowing. The state we call realization is simply being oneself, not knowing anything or becoming anything. If one has realized, one is that which alone is and which alone has always been. One cannot describe that state. One can only be that. Of course, we loosely talk of self-realization, for want of a better term. How to 'real-ize' or make real that which alone is real?

Sri Ramana Maharshi

Before man attempts to solve the secrets of the Universe without, he should master the Universe within — the Kingdom of the Self.

Yogi Ramacharaka

You cannot make yourself feel something you do not feel, but you can make yourself do right in spite of your feelings.

Pearl S. Buck

The self cannot be found in books. You have to find it for yourself, within yourself.

Sri Ramana Maharshi

Asian Words of Inspiration

We think that there is something hiding our reality and that it must be destroyed before the reality is gained. It is ridiculous. A day will dawn when you will yourself laugh at your past efforts. That which will be on the day you laugh is also here and now.

Sri Ramana Maharshi

Like two golden birds perched on the selfsame tree, intimate friends, the ego and the Self dwell in the same body. The former eats the sweet and sour fruits of the tree of life, while the latter looks on in detachment.

The Upanishads

Light the lamp within; strive hard to attain wisdom. Become pure and innocent, and you will be free from birth and death.

The Dhammapada

All will come as you go on. Take the first step first. All blessings come from within. Turn within. "I am" you know. Be with it all the time you can spare, until you revert to it spontaneously. There is no simpler and easier way.

Nisargadatta Maharaj

The moment the slave resolves that he will no longer be a slave his fetters fall. Freedom and slavery are mental states.

Mohandas Karamchand (Mahatma) Gandhi

Asian Words of Inspiration

If you look into your own heart and you find nothing wrong there, what is there to worry about or to fear?

Confucius

The essence of Buddhism is not meditation or liberation from *samsara*. It is *kensho*, "seeing into your nature."

Awa Kenzo

In every moment you only have one real choice: to be aware of the Self or to identify with the body and the mind.

Annamalai Swami

Being the source of both, the self is beyond both knowledge and power. The observable is in the mind. The nature of the self is pure awareness, pure witnessing, unaffected by the presence or absence of knowledge or liking. Have your being outside this body of birth and death and all your problems will be solved. They exist because you believe yourself born to die. Undeceive yourself and be free. You are not a person.

Nisargadatta Maharaj

Awareness is ever there. It need not be realized. Open the shutter of the mind, and it will be flooded with light.

Nisargadatta Maharaj

Asian Words of Inspiration

Oh you who are a copy of the divine book, you who are the mirror of the royal beauty, nothing exists in the world but you. Search within yourself for what you desire: it is you.

Rumi

The eyes of a saint are always concentrated on the supreme Self. The minute he is aware of himself, sainthood is lost.

Neem Karoli Baba

Do not seek any rules or method of worship. Say whatever your pained heart chooses.

Rumi

Fighting the ego, the mind is precisely what the ego wants. You cannot fight the mind. You cannot suppress the ego. Fighting, resisting, controlling it is an impossible action. What is really needed is a negative or feminine action. That is to yield, to allow things to be as they are.

Ramesh S. Balsekar

Intellect is essential to bring a sentient being to the point of take-off into Self-realization, which is the point where intellect recognizes that it cannot know its own source.

Ramesh S. Balsekar

Asian Words of Inspiration

When the ego dies, the soul awakes.
>Mohandas Karamchand (Mahatma) Gandhi

I have lived on the lip of insanity, wanting to know reasons, knocking on a door. It opens. I've been knocking from the inside!
>Rumi

O seeker, these thoughts have such power over you. From nothing you become sad. From nothing you become happy. You are burning in the flames but I will not let you out until you are fully baked, fully wise, and fully yourself.
>Rumi

One who doubts everything should also doubt one's own conclusions in order to be a consistent skeptic.
>Swami Krishnananda Saraswati

Realizing one's true nature requires no phenomenal efforts. Enlightenment cannot be attained or forced; it can only happen. So long as there is a pseudo-entity considering itself a seeker working toward enlightenment, for just so long will enlightenment be prevented from happening.
>Ramesh S. Balsekar

Asian Words of Inspiration

Discover all you are not. Body, feelings, thoughts, ideas, time, space, being, and not-being, this or that — nothing concrete or abstract you can point out to is you. A mere verbal statement will not do — you may repeat a formula endlessly without any result whatsoever. You must watch yourself continuously — particularly your mind – moment by moment, missing nothing. This witnessing is essential for the separation of the self from the not-self.

Nisargadatta Maharaj

Realizing one's true nature requires no phenomenal efforts. Enlightenment cannot be attained or forced; it can only happen. So long as there is a pseudo-entity considering itself a seeker working toward enlightenment, for just so long will enlightenment be prevented from happening.

Ramesh S. Balsekar

Everywhere is Consciousness and everywhere is Home. "Everywhere" is but a small corner of your heart. You are that vast. There is no travel because you are always Home. Surrender your ego and you are Home.

Hariwansh Lal (Papaji) Poonja

Asian Words of Inspiration

Somewhere in you you know the truth and when you stubbornly insist that you don't know then you go up and down.

Swami Amar Jyoti

Anger and lust make a man squint; they cloud the spirit so it strays from truth. When self-interest appears, virtue hides: a hundred veils rise between the heart and the eye.

Rumi

Approaching the self is like walking on a razor's edge: Two cannot go there, you can't even bring your mind or a thought. So the only one who can help you is self. Anything that touches this flame becomes flame. Touch a sage and you become a sage, knowing self you see only self and this self is your teacher.

Hariwansh Lal (Papaji) Poonja

Culture of the mind must be subservient to the heart.

Mohandas Karamchand (Mahatma) Gandhi

He who knows others is learned; He who knows himself is wise.

Lao-Tzu

Asian Words of Inspiration

We carry inside us the wonders we seek outside us.

Buddha

Are you still thinking, looking, living, as from an imaginary phenomenal center? As long as you do that you can never recognize your freedom.

Wei Wu Wei

Use your mind. Remember. Observe. You are not different from others. Most of their experiences are valid for you too. Think clearly, deeply, go into the entire structure of your desires and their ramifications. They are a most important part of your mental and emotional make-up and powerfully affect your actions. Remember, you cannot abandon what you do not know. To go beyond yourself, you must know yourself.

Nisargadatta Maharaj

The idea of time is only in your mind. It is not in the Self. There is no time for the Self. Time arises as an idea after the ego arises. But you are the Self beyond time and space. You exist even in the absence of time and space.

Sri Ramana Maharshi

Asian Words of Inspiration

If you would deny the ego and scorch it by ignoring it, you would be free. If you accept it, it will impose limitations on you and throw you into a vain struggle to transcend them. To be the Self that you really are is the only means to realize the bliss that is ever yours.

Sri Ramana Maharshi

The mind is everything. What you think you become.

Buddha

All that we are is the result of what we have thought.

Buddha

You are not a drop in the ocean. You are the entire ocean in a drop.

Rumi

I am learning to be patient and compassionate with myself as I gain the courage to be true to myself.

Shakti Gawain

If you are eager to be nothing before you know who you are, you rob yourself of your true being. Until you understand nothingness you will never know true faith.

Rumi

Asian Words of Inspiration

To get rid of all suffering and all deaths stay as Source. There nothing exists, all is perfection, Fullness, and that is your nature. You are already That and will always be That. All these notions like "I am the body" and "I am ego" give you suffering. These notions you have been told and there was a time when all these notions did not exist. You were perfect and even now you are perfect. Get rid of all these notions that have been dumped on your head. Shake them off! Shake them off and you will see who you are at this present moment. What notion is in your mind right now?

Hariwansh Lal (Papaji) Poonja

In the center of the circle is seen the perfect formula of creation. A perfect equation between Light and phenomena. Get to the Source first and open your eyes; the whole phenomena is Light-full. You'll see then there never was darkness. Stream, know thy Source. Ray, know thy Center. Man, know thy Self; that will be the real solution.

Swami Amar Jyoti

You are searching the world for treasure but the real treasure is yourself.

Rumi

Asian Words of Inspiration

Once you conquer your selfish self, all your darkness will change to light.

Rumi

There is nothing to gain. Abandon all imaginings and know yourself as you are. Self-knowledge is detachment. All craving is due to a sense of insufficiency. When you know that you lack nothing, that all there is, is you and yours, desire ceases.

Nisargadatta Maharaj

Knowing others is wisdom; knowing the self is enlightenment.

Tao Te Ching

The idol of your self is the mother of all idols. The material idol is only a snake; while this inner idol is a dragon. It is easy to break an idol, but to regard the self as easy to subdue is a mistake.

Rumi

The most important point is to accept yourself and stand on your own two feet.

Shunryu Suzuki

Asian Words of Inspiration

Only those who are able to see their own face without a mirror will be able to see their true nature. What kind of seeing is this? To see without the mirror is to see not with eyes seeing objects but as THAT which sees. It is the in-seeing or insight by Consciousness itself in which there is no one who is seeing.

Ramesh S. Balsekar

Be interested in yourself beyond all experience, be with yourself, love yourself; the ultimate security is found only in self-knowledge. The main thing is earnestness. Be honest with yourself and nothing will betray you. Virtues and powers are mere tokens for children to play with. They are useful in the world, but do not take you out of it. To go beyond, you need alert immobility, quiet attention.

Nisargadatta Maharaj

You are fighting with yourself. You have to resolve it, not fight with it. Resolve it, resolve, dissolve, solve.

Swami Amar Jyoti

Enlightenment, joy, and peace can never be given to you by another. The well is inside you.

Thich Nhat Hanh

Asian Words of Inspiration

Yesterday I was clever, so I wanted to change the world. Today I am wise, so I am changing myself.

Rumi

Satsang will take you out of suffering because it shows you the Silence that you have always been. *Satsang* is abiding as your Self, not as "I-am-so-and-so."

Hariwansh Lal (Papaji) Poonja

The idol of yourself is the mother of all idols.

Rumi

You are misled if you think the self is easy to subdue.

Rumi

You are very powerful, provided you know how powerful you are.

Yogi Bhajan

Asian Words of Inspiration

Asian Words of Inspiration

Mindfulness and Being Present

Mindfulness, an essential practice within Buddhism, is the intentional, accepting, and non-judgmental focus and concentration of one's attention on the thoughts, emotions, sensations, and surrounding environment being experienced in the present moment.

It is also practiced outside the Buddhist tradition through therapeutic applications to reduce stress, anxiety, and even symptoms of depression. Some even view mindfulness as a method for developing wisdom.

There are many studies showing that mindfulness improves both mental and physical health. Benefits include relieving stress, treating heart disease, lowering blood pressure, reducing chronic pain, improving sleep, and alleviating gastrointestinal problems.

There is little doubt that increasing one's capacity for mindfulness brings forth many attitudes that contribute to a satisfied life. This is not surprising, since being mindful and more fully present makes it easier to cherish the pleasures of life as they are occurring.

Asian Words of Inspiration

As these Asian words of wisdom below will exhibit, focusing on the present and concentrating on the here and now results in fewer worries about the future or regrets over the past. It also enables the formation of deeper connections with others.

I hope that by reflecting on the quotations and phrases in this section that you will bring forth greater mindfulness and presence in your life.

You are the self, here and now. Leave the mind alone, stand aware and unconcerned and you will realize that to stand alert but detached, watching events come and go, is an aspect of your real nature.

Nisargadatta Maharaj

Stillness means 'being free from thoughts' and yet aware.
Sri Ramana Maharshi

Silence of the mind that is the result of a deep understanding — that meditation is a natural, spontaneous meditation that just happens.

Ramesh S. Balsekar

Asian Words of Inspiration

Meditation is not sitting and fidgeting, daydreaming, worrying, or fantasizing. It means watching, calmly observing the mind itself. Calm observation makes the mind itself calmer.

Swami Rama

Present moment awareness is powerful because the future is created by our actions in the present. We cannot take action in the past or in the future. Past and future are born in the imagination. Only the present, which is awareness, is real and eternal.

Deepak Chopra

Psychoanalysis, that is essential to understand the structure of the mind, is part of Yoga itself. Yoga is the highest form of self-analysis.

Swami Krishnananda Saraswati

You are the Self, here and now. Leave the mind alone, stand aware and unconcerned, and you will realize that to stand alert but detached, watching events come and go, is an aspect of your real nature.

Nisargadatta Maharaj

Asian Words of Inspiration

Yoga is a way to freedom. By its constant practice, we can free ourselves from fear, anguish and loneliness.

Indra Devi

If you cannot find the truth right where you are, where else do you expect to find it?

Dōgen Zenji

Set your mind,
Stop your mind,
With no mind,
With your Mind,
Shine!

Awa Kenzo
Zen Bow, Zen Arrow

Do not dwell in the past, do not dream of the future, concentrate the mind on the present moment.

Buddha

Meditation is not a way of making your mind quiet. It is a way of entering into the quiet that is already there – buried under the 50,000 thoughts the average person thinks every day.

Deepak Chopra

Asian Words of Inspiration

When the mind is stilled there is no desire to think any more. We become free when there are no clouds covering the horizon of our purified consciousness.

Mouni Sadhu

Meditation is not a tension, it is not a strain. One is never tired of meditation. It is relaxation — how you can be tired of it? It is deep rest, it is utter restfulness. One is available to everything; nothing can distract you.

Osho

Meditation is painful in the beginning but it bestows immortal bliss and supreme joy in the end.

Swami Sivananda

It should be as easy to expel an obnoxious thought from your mind as it is to shake a stone out of your shoe; and till a man can do that it is just nonsense to talk about his ascendancy over Nature, and all the rest of it.

Yogi Ramacharaka

Stillness of mind comes from giving up all attachments except that attachment to Self.

Hariwansh Lal (Papaji) Poonja

Asian Words of Inspiration

Training the mind helps one to bear sorrows and bereavement with courage and finally these do not affect such a wise one.

Sri Ramana Maharshi

Mind is by nature restless. Begin liberating it from restlessness: give it peace, make it free from distractions, train it to look inward. Make this a habit. This is done by ignoring the external world and removing the obstacles in the way to mental peace.

Sri Ramana Maharshi

Love is seeing God in the person next to us, and meditation is seeing God within us.

Sri Sri Ravi Shankar

Meditation is nothing but putting the mind aside, putting the mind out of the way, and bringing a witnessing which is always there but hidden underneath the mind. This witnessing will reach to your center, and once you have become enlightened, then there is no problem. Then bring the mind in tune with you.

Osho

Asian Words of Inspiration

Purity of mind and idleness are incompatible.

                        Mohandas Karamchand (Mahatma) Gandhi

May our heart's garden of awakening bloom with hundreds of flowers.

                        Thich Nhat Hanh

The more man meditates upon good thoughts, the better will be his world and the world at large.

                        Confucius

The one and only reality can be experienced only by those who attain peace by stilling the mind's movements: it is beyond the reach of those whose minds are restless.

                        Sri Ramana Maharshi

Until the storm of conceptual thinking subsides and the mind learns to rest in a fasting state, one's true nature must remain unknown and inaccessible.

                        Ramesh S. Balsekar

With repeated meditation practice the expanse of the visible universe with all its qualities dissolves to nothing, to where there is only health and great joy.

                        Lalla

Asian Words of Inspiration

If we know the divine art of concentration, if we know the divine art of meditation, if we know the divine art of contemplation, easily and consciously we can unite the inner world and the outer world.

Sri Chinmoy

When the mind is pure you will see Self in all beings. Purify the mind by removing all concepts, especially the concept of purity. Then Self reveals itself to the empty mind that is consciousness.

Hariwansh Lal (Papaji) Poonja

It is vital to realize that understanding is all, that there is no question of altering, or amending what is, and that therefore the question of any method or technique for "attaining" enlightenment is totally irrelevant.

Ramesh S. Balsekar

"Put yourself in someone's shoes" is a common phrase but it is not a common thing that we do every day. We are, most of the time, self-centered, especially in this modern, fast-paced life. It is only when we stop for a moment and give our time to others that we realize the true meaning of empathy.

Abdul Manan Bin Hassan

Asian Words of Inspiration

The function of the mind is studied in analysis and all the various mental functions have to be studied, and it requires time. It is a long process of analysis undertaken leisurely. You need a guide for this because you are studying yourself and therefore will be prone to justifications of your own way of thinking. You hold an opinion, because you are sure that it is right. But it may not be so in the final analysis that we have undertaken. Therefore, a personal guide is needed, because it is better to have two heads than one. Especially in the advanced states of meditation, you need the guidance of a competent person.

Swami Krishnananda Saraswati

Meditation is good. One can attain a pure mind by one-pointedness and detachment. Meditate on one point and you will know.

Neem Karoli Baba

If I ask you what is the taste of your mouth, all you can do is to say: it is neither sweet nor bitter nor sour nor astringent; it is what remains when all these tastes are not. Similarly, when all distinctions and reactions are no more, what remains is reality, simple and solid.

Nisargadatta Maharaj

Asian Words of Inspiration

To meditate you don't have to have any objective, which means you don't have any expectation at all. In these moments you don't find Reality, the Reality finds you. Just sit quietly for a moment.

Ramesh S. Balsekar

Men cannot see their reflection in running water, but only in still water.

Chuang Tzu

The degree of freedom from unwanted thoughts and the degree of concentration on a single thought are the measures to gauge spiritual progress.

Sri Ramana Maharshi

An untroubled mind, no longer seeking to consider what is right and what is wrong, a mind beyond judgements watches and understands.

Buddha

The unchangeable can only be realized in silence. Once realized, it will deeply affect the changeable, itself remaining unaffected.

Nisargadatta Maharaj

Asian Words of Inspiration

First, lay down your head then one by one let go of all distractions. Embrace the light and let it guide you beyond the winds of desire. There you will find a spring and nourished by its sweet waters like a tree you will bear fruit forever.

Rumi

When both the rational and intuitive planes of mind are allowed full operation, they get superimposed on each other resulting in a fasting of the mind or NO-MIND state. This is the most alert state in which the mind can find itself because of the total freedom in which it can operate — a beautiful, natural blending of discipline and spontaneity.

Ramesh S. Balsekar

Each one has a concept of the Ultimate Being; on that you concentrate. The word "ultimate" implies the finality of it, and there is nothing above it. When you ask for it, you need not ask for anything else. On that you fix your mind. This is the whole of religion, philosophy, and yoga.

Swami Krishnananda Saraswati

It is only in the depths of silence that the voice of God can be heard.

Sai Baba

Asian Words of Inspiration

All meditations are nothing but efforts to bring you to the present. When you live in the present moment, with no past hanging around you, with no future projection, you are free from life and death, you are free from body and mind. You are free — simply free — you are freedom.

Osho

The secret of health for both mind and body is not to mourn for the past, not to worry about the future, or not to anticipate troubles, but to live in the present moment wisely and earnestly.

Buddha

The technique to return to your source is very simple. The outside attachments do not allow sitting still and meditating. So avoid, for some time, all outside attachments like you do when you sleep and have a very peaceful night. Practice this in the daytime. The instant in which you forget all your outside attachments will be the taste of tremendous love and happiness. Then slowly you will stop looking outside until the outside and the inside are the same causing both to cease to exist.

Hariwansh Lal (Papaji) Poonja

Asian Words of Inspiration

The transcendental understanding of which the sages speak cannot be transferred or transmitted. It must happen in the effortless silence of the phenomenal void, and there is no way to get it through exertion or effort.

Ramesh S. Balsekar

Meditation will drop all the masks. It is a search for the original face.

Osho

In the attitude of silence the soul finds the path in a clearer light, and what is elusive and deceptive resolves itself into crystal clearness. Our life is a long and arduous quest after Truth.

Mohandas Karamchand (Mahatma) Gandhi

The disease is simple and the remedy equally simple. It is your mind only that makes you insecure and unhappy. Anticipation makes you insecure, memory makes you unhappy. Stop misusing your mind and all will be well with you. You need not set it right. It will set itself right, as soon as you give up all concern with the past and the future and live entirely in the now.

Nisargadatta Maharaj

Asian Words of Inspiration

To understand the immeasurable, the mind must be extraordinarily quiet, still.

Jiddu Krishnamurti

Be quiet, make no effort and you will know who you are!

Hariwansh Lal (Papaji) Poonja

A quiet mind is all you need. All else will happen rightly, once your mind is quiet. As the sun on rising makes the world active, so does self-awareness affect changes in the mind. In the light of calm and steady self-awareness, inner energies wake up and work miracles without any effort on your part.

Nisargadatta Maharaj

Solitude is in the mind of man. One might be in the thick of the world and maintain serenity of mind. Such a one is in solitude. Another may stay in a forest, but still be unable to control his mind. Such a man cannot be said to be in solitude. Solitude is a function of the mind. A man attached to desires cannot get solitude wherever he may be, whereas a detached man is always in solitude.

Sri Ramana Maharshi

Asian Words of Inspiration

All effort at controlling thoughts, appetites, and desires cannot but strengthen them along with the ego. Whatever has to go must fall off by itself. All that you are concerned with, all that you are, is the impersonal functioning of understanding. So let that understanding work through witnessing without judgment, knowing that there is nothing else that you can do.

Ramesh S. Balsekar

What is the undercurrent which vivifies the mind, enables it to do all this work? It is the Self. So that is the real source of your activity. Simply be aware of it during your work and do not forget it. Contemplate in the background of your mind even whilst working. To do that, do not hurry, take your own time. Keep the remembrance of your real nature alive, even while working, and avoid haste which causes you to forget. Be deliberate. Practice meditation to still the mind and cause it to become aware of its true relationship to the Self which supports it. Do not imagine it is you who are doing the work. Think that it is the underlying current which is doing it. Identify yourself with the current. If you work unhurriedly, recollectedly, your work or service need not be a hindrance.

Sri Ramana Maharshi

Asian Words of Inspiration

Dispassion doesn't mean to separate oneself from people but to understand that this world is not real. Dispassion is attachment to God. When a yogi gets dispassion, he sometimes gets the thought to leave the body. But to leave the body by being in the body is real dispassion. Dispassion is a state of mine in which one can live in desires without desire.

Baba Hari Dass

How can an unsteady mind make itself steady? Of course it cannot. It is the nature of the mind to roam about. All you can do is to shift the focus of consciousness beyond the mind.

Nisargadatta Maharaj

To be aware is to be awake. Unaware means asleep. You are aware anyhow, you need not try to be. What you need is to be aware of being aware. Be aware deliberately and consciously, broaden and deepen the field of awareness. You are always conscious of the mind, but you are not aware of yourself as being conscious.

Nisargadatta Maharaj

When you realize there is nothing lacking, the whole world belongs to you.

Lao-Tzu

Asian Words of Inspiration

The mind turned inwards is the Self; turned outwards it becomes the ego and all the world. Cotton made into various clothes we call by various names. Gold made into various ornaments, we call by various names. But all the clothes are cotton and all the ornaments gold. The one is real, the many are mere names and forms.

Sri Ramana Maharshi

Silence is the great teacher, and to learn its lessons you must pay attention to it. There is no substitute for the creative inspiration, knowledge, and stability that come from knowing how to contact your core of inner silence.

Deepak Chopra

Realization is nothing to be gained afresh; it is already there. All that is necessary is to get rid of the thought 'I have not realized.' Stillness or peace is realization. There is no moment when the Self is not. So long as there is doubt or the feeling of non-realization, the attempt should be made to rid oneself of these thoughts. They are due to the identification of the Self with the not-Self. When the not-Self disappears, the Self alone remains. To make room, it is enough that objects be removed. Room is not brought in from elsewhere.

Sri Ramana Maharshi

Asian Words of Inspiration

What are you wanting, finally? On that you have to fix your attention. Whether you call it *hatha* yoga or *kriya* yoga or anything else is not important. Fix your consciousness on your concept of final reality, and it shall reward you. You have to decide yourself what is ultimately real, in yourself or in the world; then fix your attention and attune your consciousness with it. This is meditation. It has no particular name.

Swami Krishnananda Saraswati

Silence of the mind is the result of a deep understanding.

Ramesh S. Balsekar

Enlightenment absorbs this universe of qualities. When that merging occurs, there is nothing but God. This is the only doctrine. There is no word for it, no mind to understand it with, no categories of transcendence or non-transcendence, no vow of silence, no mystical attitude. There is no Shiva and no Shakti in enlightenment, and if there is something that remains, that whatever-it-is is the only teaching.

Lalla

Each moment contains a hundred messages from God.

Rumi

Asian Words of Inspiration

Meditation is not evasion. It is a serene encounter with reality.

Thich Nhat Hanh

There is no need to avoid false thoughts or seek true ones because all thought is spontaneous, involuntary, and without substance. It is neither to be accepted nor rejected but ignored so that it disappears as spontaneously as it appeared.

Ramesh S. Balsekar

That pure consciousness which is the reality, and which shines without a break, as "I AM" when the mind becomes calm, is the supreme bliss.

Sri Ramana Maharshi

If you could only keep quiet, clear of memories and expectations, you would be able to discern the beautiful pattern of events. It is your restlessness that causes chaos.

Nisargadatta Maharaj

Knowing that the intrusion of the mind is a natural process, that it has to happen, that understanding itself will return one to the witnessing.

Ramesh S. Balsekar

Asian Words of Inspiration

Forget the known, but remember that you are the knower. Don't be all the time immersed in your experiences. Remember that you are beyond the experiencer, ever unborn and deathless. In remembering it, the quality of pure knowledge will emerge, the light of unconditional awareness.

Nisargadatta Maharaj

Time is in the mind, space is in the mind. The law of cause and effect is also a way of thinking. In reality all is here and now and all is one. Multiplicity and diversity are in the mind only.

Nisargadatta Maharaj

Spiritual advancement is not to be measured by one's display of outward powers, but solely by the depth of his bliss in meditation.

Paramahansa Yogananda

Thought is absent in seeing things intuitively. When you perceive directly, there is no thinking. When you think you understand, you don't. You don't think that you are alive, you know that you are alive.

Ramesh S. Balsekar

Asian Words of Inspiration

To enjoy good health, to bring true happiness to one's family, to bring peace to all, one must first discipline and control one's own mind. If a man can control his mind he can find the way to Enlightenment, and all wisdom and virtue will naturally come to him.

Buddha

If you want to reach a state of bliss, then go beyond your ego and the internal dialogue. Make a decision to relinquish the need to control, the need to be approved, and the need to judge. Those are the three things the ego is doing all the time. It's very important to be aware of them every time they come up.

Deepak Chopra

As it rises so it falls. Make effort and it rises. Stop effort and it falls. Make the choice! Stay a simple natural Being without thought or doership. Out of nothing you can do anything and not leave footprints. No intention is no limitation, just stay quiet, simply do not stir a thought. Not activating the mind is to not externalize. There is no way or method, just keep out of the way. The revelation of the Self will occur only when you do not interfere. Keeping quiet is giving time to this love and beauty. Stay as Such.

Hariwansh Lal (Papaji) Poonja

Asian Words of Inspiration

The secret of health for both mind and body is not to mourn for the past, nor to worry about the future, but to live the present moment wisely and earnestly.

Buddha

Last night I begged the Wise One to tell me the secret of the world. Gently, gently he whispered, "Be quiet, the secret cannot be spoken, it is wrapped in silence."

Rumi

Self-enquiry is the direct path to Self-realization or enlightenment. The only way to make the mind cease its outward activities is to turn it inward. By steady and continuous investigation into the nature of the mind, the mind itself gets transformed into that to which it owes its own existence.

Ramesh S. Balsekar

I have stilled my restless mind, and my heart is radiant, for in That-ness I have seen beyond That-ness, in company I have seen the Comrade Himself. Living in bondage, I have set myself free. I have broken away from the clutch of all narrowness. I have attained the unattainable, and my heart is colored with the color of love.

Kabir

Asian Words of Inspiration

Breathing in I calm body and mind. Breathing out, I smile.
Thich Nhat Hahn

Don't make any effort. Stay quiet and the noisy surface dialogues will cease. Then the substratum will rise up to the top. It is simple. Follow this.
Hariwansh Lal (Papaji) Poonja

If we know the divine art of concentration, if we know the divine art of meditation, if we know the divine art of contemplation, easily and consciously we can unite the inner world and the outer world.
Sri Chinmoy

Generally we waste our lives, distracted from our true selves, in endless activity. Meditation is the way to bring us back to ourselves, where we can really experience and taste our full being.
Sogyal Rinpoche

There is a way between voice and presence where information flows. In disciplined silence it opens. With wandering talk it closes.
Rumi

Asian Words of Inspiration

The state of craving for anything blocks all deeper experience. Nothing of value can happen to a mind that knows exactly what it wants, for nothing the mind can visualize and want is of much value.

Nisargadatta Maharaj

Enlightenment is merely an understanding in which there is no comprehender. It is a surrender in which there is no one to surrender anything.

Ramesh S. Balsekar

Control the mind as a slave and it will be very helpful to you. Know this trick from the outer Guru. Control the slave, love the slave, keep it quiet. Don't trouble the mind and don't let it trouble you. This is how to control the mind.

Hariwansh Lal (Papaji) Poonja

To a mind that is still, the whole universe surrenders.

Lao-Tzu

The quieter you become, the more you are able to hear.

Rumi

Asian Words of Inspiration

To make the right choices in life, you have to get in touch with your soul. To do this, you need to experience solitude, which most people are afraid of, because in the silence you hear the truth and know the solutions.

Deepak Chopra

Feelings come and go like clouds in a windy sky. Conscious breathing is my anchor.

Thich Nhat Hanh

Let silence take you to the core of life.

Rumi

Each minute we spend worrying about the future and regretting the past is a minute we miss in our appointment with life.

Thich Nhat Hanh

Empty your mind of all thoughts. Let your heart be at peace.

Lao-Tzu

Discard every self-seeking motive as soon as it is seen and you need not search for truth; truth will find you.

Nisargadatta Maharaj

Asian Words of Inspiration

People often ask how the mind is controlled. I say to them "Show me the mind and then you will know what to do." The fact is that the mind is only a bundle of thoughts. How can you extinguish it by the thought of doing so or by a desire? Your thoughts and desires are part and parcel of the mind. The mind is simply fattened by new thoughts rising up. Therefore it is foolish to attempt to kill the mind by means of the mind. The only way of doing it is to find its source and hold on to it. The mind will then fade away of its own accord.

            Sri Ramana Maharshi

You can be seen sitting for hours, palms turned to heaven, eyes shut, your breath even as it exits your nose. Your attention is focused. You've been doing this for a while now. You're getting good at it. At first you could barely sit five minutes. Now you can disappear for hours. Why do you come back?

                   Ram Tzu

The joy that is in Revelation is nowhere else. No amount of perception, thinking, projecting, planning, doing efforts, achieving, ever will give you that joy, that radiance that Revelation does.

              Swami Amar Jyoti

Asian Words of Inspiration

Stillness and tranquility set things in order in the universe.

Lao-Tzu

When the mind is quiet, we come to know ourselves as the pure witness. We withdraw from the experience and its experiencer and stand apart in pure awareness that is between and beyond the two. The personality, based on self-identification, on imagining oneself to be something: "I am this, I am that," continues, but only as a part of the objective world. Its identification with the witness snaps.

Nisargadatta Maharaj

Breathing in, I calm my body.
Breathing out, I smile.
Dwelling in the present
I know this is a wonderful moment.

Thich Nhat Hanh

Everything inside and around us wants to reflect itself in us. We don't have to go anywhere to obtain the truth. We only need to be still and things will reveal themselves in the still water of our heart.

Thich Nhat Hanh

Asian Words of Inspiration

Seeking is not a matter of comprehension; it is a matter of intuitive apprehension. But it has to be arrived at through the intellect.

Ramesh S. Balsekar

What is here is also there; what is there, is also here. Who sees multiplicity but not the one indivisible Self must wander on and on from death to death.

The Upanishads

Asian Words of Inspiration

Peace and Peacefulness

The realm of the spirit is inner peace.

This occurs when your mind stops its incessant chatter, your heart is not anxious, and your energy streams as naturally (and as life giving) as your breathing. This is a state of flow, not repose, and can take place anytime or anywhere, even when you are fully engaged in an activity. It happens when your mind, spirit, and body are in perfect harmony.

Unfortunately, our minds constantly get in the way and prevent this state of flow from happening. Our worries, concerns, expectations, hopes, desires — each and every thought — block flow from happening.

However, when we truly align our human and spiritual selves, we need not fear any human experience, including death. Nor need we fear the loss of any worldly possessions, including friendships, relationships, and material belongings. After all, as eternal spiritual beings, we can let go of anything and everything we possess or experience in this world. Doing so does not impact our ability to spiritually continue to exist, experience, and grow.

Asian Words of Inspiration

Knowing this releases us from attachment. We do not need to be attached to anything or anyone, except ourselves. When you truly know this, life becomes blissful and peaceful, regardless of future events, experiences, or outcomes.

May reflecting upon the varied thoughts in this section bring a greater level of peace and peacefulness into your life.

Do not speak unless you can improve on silence.

Buddha

All sorrows are destroyed upon attainment of tranquility. The intellect of such a tranquil person soon becomes completely steady.

Bhagavad Gita

Peace will not come out of a clash of arms but out of justice lived and done by unarmed nations in the face of odds.

Mohandas Karamchand (Mahatma) Gandhi

Asian Words of Inspiration

The man who has peace in his soul has all the wisdom of the gods.

                                        Paramahansa Yogananda

Each one has to find his peace from within. And peace to be real must be unaffected by outside circumstances.

                        Mohandas Karamchand (Mahatma) Gandhi

Permanent good can never be the outcome of untruth and violence.

                        Mohandas Karamchand (Mahatma) Gandhi

If we have no peace, it is because we have forgotten that we belong to each other.

                                                Mother Teresa

Peace is inside you. Wherever you go, peace goes with you. When you climb on a bus, peace goes with you. When you are fighting, peace goes with you. When you are asleep, peace is within you.

                                                      Prem Rawat

Peace is the inner nature of man. If you find it within yourself, you will then find it everywhere.

                                        Sri Ramana Maharshi

Asian Words of Inspiration

I have not the qualification for teaching my philosophy of life. I have barely qualifications for practicing the philosophy I believe. I am but a poor struggling soul yearning to be wholly good, wholly truthful and wholly non-violent in thought, word and deed, but ever failing to reach the ideal which I know to be true.

                      Mohandas Karamchand (Mahatma) Gandhi

Peace is its own reward.

                      Mohandas Karamchand (Mahatma) Gandhi

It is possible to live in peace.

                      Mohandas Karamchand (Mahatma) Gandhi

Inward calm cannot be maintained unless physical strength is constantly and intelligently replenished.

                      Buddha

Emotional reactions, born of ignorance or inadvertence, are never justified. Seek a clear mind and a clean heart. All you need is to keep quietly alert, enquiring into the real nature of yourself. This is the only way to peace.

                      Nisargadatta Maharaj

Asian Words of Inspiration

When a man dwells on the objects of sense, he creates an attraction for them; attraction develops into desire, and desire breeds anger. Anger induces delusion; delusion, loss of memory; through loss of memory, reason is shattered and loss of reason leads to destruction. But the self-controlled soul who moves amongst sense-objects free from either attachment or repulsion wins eternal peace. Having attained peace, he becomes free from misery; for when the mind gains peace, right discrimination follows.

Bhagavad Gita

Conquest breeds hatred, for the conquered live in sorrow. Let us be neither conqueror nor conquered, and live in peace and joy.

The Dhammapada

You are what all happenings happen in. What happens must happen so remain unaffected as Peace. Be peaceful and this Peace will spread. What rises from Peace is Peace and what rises from confusion is confusion. So Be Peace and give this to the Universe, it is all you should do. Even thinking "I am Peace" disturbs this Peace, so just be Quiet, be as you are.

Hariwansh Lal (Papaji) Poonja

Asian Words of Inspiration

Peace comes from within. Do not seek it without.

Buddha

You will find peace, or rather peace will find itself, when there is the perception that what you are searching for cannot be found.

Ramesh S. Balsekar

Non-violence is not a garment to be put on and off at will. Its seat is in the heart, and it must be inseparable part of our very being.

Mohandas Karamchand (Mahatma) Gandhi

All sorrows are destroyed upon attainment of tranquility. The intellect of such a tranquil person soon becomes completely steady.

Bhagavad Gita

The Teacher will not be recognized by the diamonds on his head or by the number of students he has. Know the Teacher to be the one whose presence gives you peace and removes all the craving, attachment, and desire.

Hariwansh Lal (Papaji) Poonja

Asian Words of Inspiration

I object to violence because when it appears to do good, the good is only temporary; the evil it does is permanent.

                Mohandas Karamchand (Mahatma) Gandhi

Within the great distress of life, a true master remains at ease.

                Awa Kenzo

A brave and passionate man will kill or be killed. A brave and calm man will always preserve life.

                Lao-Tzu

When you have made peace with your mind you have made peace with the whole world. Do not try to control your world, just make peace with the world in your mind.

                Swami Amar Jyoti

If you have inner peace, nobody can force you to be a slave to the outer reality.

                Sri Chinmoy

Many people think excitement is happiness. But when you are excited you are not peaceful. True happiness is based on peace.

                Thich Nhat Hanh

Asian Words of Inspiration

Those who are free of resentful thoughts surely find peace.

Buddha

When you think everything is someone else's fault, you will suffer a lot. When you realize that everything springs only from yourself, you will learn both peace and joy.

Dalai Lama

If there is peace in your mind you will find peace with everybody. If your mind is agitated you will find agitation everywhere. So first find peace within and you will see this inner peace reflected everywhere else. You are this peace! You are happiness, find out. Where else will you find peace if not within you?

Hariwansh Lal (Papaji) Poonja

There is a desert I long to be walking, a wide emptiness, peace beyond any understanding of it.

Rumi

You are seeking joy and peace in far-off places. But the spring of joy is in your heart. The haven of peace is in yourself.

Sai Baba

Asian Words of Inspiration

Do not let the behavior of others destroy your inner peace.
Dalai Lama

To educate people for peace, we can use words or we can speak with our lives.
Thich Nhat Hanh

We can never obtain peace in the outer world until we make peace with ourselves.
Dalai Lama

As we cultivate peace and happiness in ourselves, we also nourish peace and happiness in those we love.
Thich Nhat Hanh

If you wish to experience peace, provide peace for another.
Dalai Lama

As the lotus rises on its stalk unsoiled by mud and water, so the wise one speaks of peace and is unstained by the opinions of the world.
Buddha

Asian Words of Inspiration

If you are depressed you are living in the past. If you are anxious you are living in the future. If you are at peace you are living in the present.

Lao-Tzu

Tension is who you think you should be. Relaxation is who you are.

Chinese Proverb

Discard all traditional standards. Leave them to the hypocrites. Only what liberates you from desire and fear and wrong ideas is good. As long as you worry about sin and virtue you will have no peace.

Nisargadatta Maharaj

I would like people to compete with me in contentment. It is the richest treasure I own.

Mohandas Karamchand (Mahatma) Gandhi

Your purpose is to be at peace, to love all beings, and to know who you are. This is the purpose of life. Slowly you will know this and get through.

Hariwansh Lal [Papaji] Poonja

Asian Words of Inspiration

Love

There are many kinds of love: parental, spousal, sexual, self, fraternal, puppy, romantic, unrequited, and dozens more. The range in the feelings of love, combined with the fact that love evolves, waxes, wanes, and sometimes dies, makes it difficult to write universally about the subject of love.

However, there is one universal truth about love that I have found. When you experience the sensation of love, you know there is a God or a Universal Supreme Being. Like the concept of a divine entity, love is an intangible concept and belief — the existence of which cannot be proven by mortal man.

Many have waxed lyrically about love, particularly the poets, playwrights, spiritual gurus and the writers of holiday gift cards. But, the best advice of all on love may have come from the actress Marlene Dietrich, "Love for the joy of loving, and not for the offerings of someone else's heart."

I think that the late Dr. David Simon, co-founder of the Chopra Center, had a keenly insightful and correct perspective on our universal desire for love, *"The human heart yearns for love, for love expands our sense of self. Love*

Asian Words of Inspiration

is a celebration of unity and a rejoicing in our essential interconnectedness. It is the doorway to freedom from isolation and alienation."

Love is a process, not an end point. Even when you fall in love with someone, this is not your final destination. Actually, falling in love is like getting onto a never-ending train ride. You are on the train of love, but neither you nor the train is stationary. As long as the train continues its journey your feeling of love remains. If the love dies out, the train stops. This love train only reaches a final destination when one of the parties passes from this earthly world, in which case the love remains with the surviving party.

I wrote earlier about the similarities between feeling love and having a belief in God or a Universal Supreme Being. Sri Sri Ravi Shankar, the spiritual leader and founder of the Art of Living Foundation, sees another connection: *"Love is seeing God in the person next to us, and meditation is seeing God within us."*

Let me now share with you some of the words of wisdom that a wide range of Asian thinkers and sages have written about love.

Asian Words of Inspiration

To understand everything is to forgive everything.
Buddha

Still your mind in me, still yourself in me, and without a doubt you shall be united with me, Lord of Love, dwelling in your heart.
Bhagavad Gita

The hunger for love is much more difficult to remove than the hunger for bread.
Mother Teresa

Let yourself be silently drawn by the stronger pull of what you really love.
Rumi

Love and compassion are necessities, not luxuries. Without them humanity cannot survive.
Dalai Lama

Your task is not to seek for love, but merely to seek and find all the barriers within yourself that you have built against it.
Rumi

Asian Words of Inspiration

Love is the unifier, the motivator and the source of joy for every being.

Sai Baba

If you want a love message to be heard, it has got to be sent out. To keep a lamp burning, we have to keep putting oil in it.

Mother Teresa

The moment you have in your heart this extraordinary thing called love and feel the depth, the delight, the ecstasy of it, you will discover that for you the world is transformed.

Jiddu Krishnamurti

Who travels for love finds a thousand miles not longer than one.

Japanese Proverb

Love does not cling; clinging is not love.

Nisargadatta Maharaj

Love is natural. Console your mind and make it listen. Love all or it is not love. Make your mind love this way and you will see the magic of this every day.

Hariwansh Lal [Papaji] Poonja

Asian Words of Inspiration

The real friendship is like fluorescence, it shines better when everything has darken.

Rabindranath Tagore

Every time you smile at someone, it is an action of love, a gift to that person, a beautiful thing.

Mother Teresa

Passionate love and a cough cannot be concealed.

Japanese Proverb

Trust is the first step to love.

Munshi Premchand

Love is a crocodile in the river of desire.

Indian Proverb

Giving love to all, feeling the love of God, seeing His presence in everyone; that is the way to live in this world.

Paramahansa Yogananda

Being deeply loved by someone gives you strength, while loving someone deeply gives you courage.

Lao-Tzu

Asian Words of Inspiration

When your heart is dark as iron, steadily polish yourself that the heart may become a mirror, a beautiful shine reflecting from within. Although iron is dark and dismal, polishing clears the darkness away.

Rumi

Through my love for you, I want to express my love for the whole cosmos, the whole of humanity, and all beings. By living with you, I want to learn to love everyone and all species. If I succeed in loving you, I will be able to love everyone and all species on Earth... This is the real message of love.

Thich Nhat Hahn

Lovers in their brief delight gamble both worlds away, a century's worth of work for one chance to surrender. Many slow growth-stages build to quick bursts of blossom. A thousand half-loves must be forsaken to take one whole heart home.

Rumi

Remember that the best relationship is one in which your love for each other exceeds your need for each other.

Dalai Lama

Asian Words of Inspiration

To love is the most important thing in life. But what do we mean by love? When you love someone because that person loves you in return, surely that is not love. To love is to have that extraordinary feeling of affection without asking anything in return.

Jiddu Krishnamurti

Sometimes we find satisfaction in self-pity. The reason is that it is our nature to find satisfaction in love; and when we are confined to ourselves we begin to love ourselves, and then self-pity arises because we feel our limitation. But the love of self always brings dissatisfaction, for the self is not made to be loved; the self is made to love. The first condition to love is to forget oneself.

Inayat Khan

You, yourself, as much as anybody in the entire universe, deserve your love and affection.

Buddha

I have found the paradox that if I love until it hurts, then there is no hurt, but only more love.

Mother Teresa

Asian Words of Inspiration

If I hold you with my emotions, you'll become a wished-for companion. If I hold you with my eyes, you'll grow old and die. So I hold you where we both mix with the infinite.

Rumi

You have two hands, two legs, and two eyes but if your heart and the Beloved are also two, what good is that? You call out, I am the lover, but these are mere words. If you see lover and Beloved as two, you either have double vision, or you can't count.

Rumi

When the sense of distinction and separation is absent, you may call it love.

Nisargadatta Maharaj

He who wants to do good knocks at the gate; he who loves finds the door open.

Rabindranath Tagore

With life as short as a half taken breath, don't plant anything but Love.

Rumi

Asian Words of Inspiration

If you can't smell the fragrance, don't come into the garden of love. If you are unwilling to undress, don't enter into the stream of truth. Stay where you are, don't come our way.

Rumi

Love others because Light is in them, not because of the person. Otherwise one day you'll miss them; you'll lose them. Love others because Light is within them. That's the Principle. Then you'll never miss them even if they die because the Principle is still existent. Embodied or disembodied it's the Principle which fulfills.

Swami Amar Jyoti

Your heart is full of fertile seeds, waiting to sprout.

Morihei Ueshiba

Let us always meet each other with smile, for the smile is the beginning of love.

Mother Teresa

However the tea is prepared, the primary ingredient is always water. While we can live without tea, we can't live without water. Likewise, we are born free of religion, but we are not born free of the need for compassion.

Dalai Lama

Asian Words of Inspiration

Judge nothing, you will be happy. Forgive everything, you will be happier. Love everything, you will be happiest.

Sri Chinmoy

Love is the water of life. Drink it down with heart and soul.

Rumi

The lover of this world is like someone in love with a wall illuminated by sunrays; he doesn't realize that the radiance and the splendor do not come from the wall but from the sun. He gives his heart to the wall and when at sunset the rays of sun disappear, he is in despair.

Rumi

Let your will burn in this fire so that it takes you nowhere else. Let your self be burned in this fire of eternity, love, and peace. Don't be afraid of this fire, it is love itself. This desire for freedom is the fire of love!

Hariwansh Lal (Papaji) Poonja

A moment's truth can and shall make the world beautiful. A moment's peace can and shall save the world. A moment's love can and shall make the world perfect.

Sri Chinmoy

Asian Words of Inspiration

The pure heart is a spotless mirror in which images of infinite beauty are reflected.

Rumi

The bamboo that bends is stronger than the oak that resists.

Japanese Proverb

Love is the absence of judgment.

Dalai Lama

If you judge people, you have no time to love them.

Mother Teresa

Gamble everything for love, if you're a true human being. If not, leave this gathering. Half-heartedness doesn't reach into majesty.

Rumi

Love is a fruit in season at all times, and in reach of every hand.

Mother Teresa

Wherever you are, and whatever you do, be in love.

Rumi

Asian Words of Inspiration

Smile at each other, smile at your wife, smile at your husband, smile at your children, smile at each other — it doesn't matter who it is — and that will help you to grow up in greater love for each other.

Mother Teresa

It is love alone that leads to right action. What brings order in the world is to love, and let love do what it will.

Jiddu Krishnamurti

Love is the vital core of the soul, and of all you see, only love is infinite.

Rumi

Our greatest strength lies in the gentleness and tenderness of our heart.

Rumi

Love is the universal order, we are the atoms; love is the ocean, we are the drops. Love has offered us a hundred proofs; we are looking for reasons. Through love, the heavens are ordered; without love, suns and moons are eclipsed. Through love what was bent is made straight; without love, what was straight becomes bent.

Rumi

Asian Words of Inspiration

Love is the highest bliss that man can attain to, for through it alone he truly knows that he is more than himself, and that he is at one with the All.

Rabindranath Tagore

Ego wants to get and forget, Love wants to give and forgive.

Sai Baba

The moment you have in your heart this extraordinary thing called love and feel the depth, the delight, the ecstasy of it, you will discover that for you the world is transformed.

Jiddu Krishnamurti

All suffering is born of desire. True love is never frustrated. How can the sense of unity be frustrated? What can be frustrated is the desire for expression. Such desire is of the mind. As with all things mental, frustration is inevitable.

Nisargadatta Maharaj

In disagreements with loved ones, deal only with the current situation. Don't bring up the past.

Dalai Lama

Asian Words of Inspiration

Asian Words of Inspiration

Your Life's Journey

Plato observed that *"the unexamined life is not worth living."*

Asian thinkers obviously agree, as sages going as far back in time as Buddha and Confucius have been examining life and providing words of wisdom on how a life journey should be lived.

Buddha, in particular, gave considerable thought to the purpose of life. His conclusion was concise: *"Your work is to discover your world and then with all your heart give yourself to it."*

This decree is interesting as it basically dictates that every individual has his or her own unique purpose in life. Thus, the instruction from Buddha needs to be individually interpreted and implemented by each of us.

Life is a miracle. One that deserves enormous respect for our own existence, as well as all other forms of life. Thinking about our respective life journeys, as the sages of Asia have long done, is much more about who we are becoming than the material things we are accumulating. Or so the wise gurus tell us.

Billions and billions of words have been written in hundreds of languages regarding the meaning of life and how to understand life's purpose. The definitions I like best come from the book **Project You: Living A Determined Life**:

> *The meaning of life is to discover, grow, develop, and enhance your unique personal gift and individual talent.*
>
> *The purpose of life is to use your unique gift and talent for the betterment of mankind, planet Earth, and the Universe of Souls.*

How you go about accomplishing this is up to you. Everything in your life is a reflection of the choices you make.

I hope the words of wisdom from Asia in this section are beneficial to you when contemplating and determining your future choices.

Asian Words of Inspiration

He who wishes to secure the good of others has already secured his own.

Confucius

In a controversy the instant we feel anger we have already ceased striving for the truth, and have begun striving for ourselves.

Buddha

Teach this triple truth to all: A generous heart, kind speech, and a life of service and compassion are the things which renew humanity.

Buddha

The two great virtues: self-control and returning kindness.

Awa Kenzo

The highest good is like water. Water gives life to the ten thousand things and does not strive. It flows in places men reject and so is like the Tao.

Lao-Tzu

Don't complain of affliction for it's a smooth-paced horse carrying you towards non-existence.

Rumi

Asian Words of Inspiration

The future depends on what we do in the present.
>Mohandas Karamchand (Mahatma) Gandhi

Life is a bridge. Cross over it, but build no house on it.
>Indian Proverb

At any moment, you have a choice, that either leads you closer to your spirit or further away from it.
>Thich Nhat Hanh

We ourselves feel that what we are doing is just a drop in the ocean. But the ocean would be less because of that missing drop.
>Mother Teresa

When clouds form in the skies we know that rain will follow but we must not wait for it. Nothing will be achieved by attempting to interfere with the future before the time is ripe. Patience is needed.
>*I Ching*

He has completed his voyage; he has gone beyond sorrow. The fetters of life have fallen from him, and he lives in full freedom.
>*The Dhammapada*

Asian Words of Inspiration

Withdrawal, aloofness, letting go is a death. To live fully, death is essential. Every ending makes a new beginning.

Nisargadatta Maharaj

The transcending of thought happens not through suppression but through the natural absence of volition or desire brought about by the recognition of one's true nature.

Ramesh S. Balsekar

To try to be true to oneself is the law of man.

Confucius

The butterfly counts not months but moments, and has time enough.

Rabindranath Tagore

Remember to light the candle of joy daily and all the gloom will disappear from your life.

Djwal Khul

Happiness depends on something or other and can be lost; freedom from everything depends on nothing and cannot be lost. Freedom from sorrow has no cause and, therefore, cannot be destroyed. Realize that freedom.

Nisargadatta Maharaj

Asian Words of Inspiration

Be happy in the moment, that's enough. Each moment is all we need, not more.

Mother Teresa

If you shut your door to all errors truth will be shut out.

Rabindranath Tagore

The longer the night lasts, the more our dreams will be.

Chinese Proverb

The real miracle is not to walk either on water or in thin air, but to walk on earth.

Thich Nhat Hanh

The desire for truth is the highest of all desires, yet, it is still a desire. All desires must be given up for the real to be. Remember that you are. This is your working capital. Rotate it and there will be much profit.

Nisargadatta Maharaj

If you cry because the sun has gone out of your life, your tears will prevent you from seeing the stars.

Rabindranath Tagore

Asian Words of Inspiration

The basic fallacy of man's search is that, instead of being the Universal Consciousness or Absolute Principle which he nominally is, he endeavors to attain an imaginary ideal happiness in his existence as a phenomenal object by trying to become something else.

Ramesh S. Balsekar

You are always thinking you are somewhere, in some place. You have to remove that idea. There is a peculiar habit of the mind asserting itself as located in some place, in a particular form, in a particular condition, etc. This must be removed so that you may know the truth.

Swami Krishnananda Saraswati

When a little bubble of joy appears in your sea of consciousness, take hold of it and keep expanding it. Meditate on it, and it will grow larger. Keep puffing at the bubble until it breaks its confining walls and becomes a sea of joy.

Paramahansa Yogananda

If you don't want anyone to know, don't do it.

Chinese Proverb

Asian Words of Inspiration

Zen opens a man's eyes to the greatest mystery as it is daily and hourly performed. It enlarges the heart to embrace eternity of time and infinity of space in its every palpitation. It makes us live in the world as if walking in the Garden of Eden.

D.T. Suzuki

You must understand the whole of life, not just one little part of it. That is why you must read, look at the skies, sing and dance, write poems, suffer and understand – for all that is life.

Jiddu Krishnamurti

If you want money more than anything, you'll be bought and sold. If you have a greed for food, you'll be a loaf of bread. This is a subtle truth: whatever you love, you are.

Rumi

There are only two things of value in this world, our time and our tears.

    Sri Srimad Bhaktivedanta Narayan Gosvami Maharaja

There is no god higher than truth.

Mohandas Karamchand (Mahatma) Gandhi

Asian Words of Inspiration

Increase of material comforts, it may be generally laid down, does not in any way whatsoever conduce to moral growth.

Mohandas Karamchand (Mahatma) Gandhi

You are what your deep, driving desire is. As your desire is, so is your will. As your will is, so is your deed. As your deed is, so is your destiny.

The Upanishads

Karma is the eternal assertion of human freedom. Our thoughts, our words, and deeds are the threads of the net which we throw around ourselves.

Swami Vivekananda

An integral being knows without going, sees without looking, and accomplishes without doing.

Lao-Tzu

This existence of ours is as transient as autumn clouds. To watch the birth and death of beings is like looking at the movements of a dance. A lifetime is like a flash of lightning in the sky, rushing by like a torrent down a steep mountain.

Buddha

Asian Words of Inspiration

Everything is based on mind, is led by mind, is fashioned by mind. If you speak and act with a polluted mind, suffering will follow you, as the wheels of the oxcart follow the footsteps of the ox. Everything is based on mind, is led by mind, is fashioned by mind. If you speak and act with a pure mind, happiness will follow you, as a shadow clings to a form.

Buddha

As human beings, our greatness lies not so much in being able to remake the world — that is the myth of the atomic age — as in being able to remake ourselves.

Mohandas Karamchand (Mahatma) Gandhi

Do not seek to follow in the footsteps of the wise. Seek what they sought.

Basho

To look at everything, trying to see what is behind it, to see it in its right light, requires divine illumination, a spiritual outlook on life. And this outlook is attained by the increase of compassion. The more compassion one has in one's heart, the more the world will begin to look different.

Inayat Khan

Asian Words of Inspiration

You will not be punished for your anger, you will be punished by your anger.

Buddha

Anger and intolerance are the enemies of correct understanding.

Mohandas Karamchand (Mahatma) Gandhi

On life's journey faith is nourishment, virtuous deeds are a shelter, wisdom is the light by day and right mindfulness is the protection by night. If a man lives a pure life, nothing can destroy him.

Buddha

He who sacrifices his conscience to ambition burns a picture to obtain the ashes.

Chinese Proverb

Hatred does not cease by hatred, but only by love; this is the eternal rule.

Buddha

One joy scatters a hundred griefs.

Chinese Proverb

Asian Words of Inspiration

Condemn none: if you can stretch out a helping hand, do so. If you cannot, fold your hands, bless your brothers, and let them go their own way.

> Swami Vivekananda

Death is not extinguishing the light; it is putting out the lamp because dawn has come.

> Rabindranath Tagore

Happiness is your nature. It is not wrong to desire it. What is wrong is seeking it outside when it is inside.

> Sri Ramana Maharshi

A good soldier is not violent. A good fighter is not angry. A good winner is not vengeful. A good employer is humble. This is known as the virtue of not striving. This is known as ability to deal with people. This since ancient times has been known as the ultimate unity with the abstract.

> Lao-Tzu

Many people excuse their own faults but judge other persons harshly. We should reverse this attitude by excusing others' shortcomings and by harshly examining our own.

> Paramahansa Yogananda

Asian Words of Inspiration

Sell your cleverness and buy bewilderment.

Rumi

Desire gives you suffering. Whenever any desire arises, you want to go near it, you want to achieve it and you do, then you are happy, right? You may think that the object made you happy, but really it is the absence of desire, that moment of emptiness, that makes you happy.

Hariwansh Lal (Papaji) Poonja

Life is suffering. Once you learn to accept that life is suffering, life will cease to be suffering.

Buddha

This world is the dream of he who sleeps. The dreamer imagines it is lasting until suddenly the dawn of Death breaks and he finds himself free from the darkness of illusion and error. Then seeing his eternal home, he will laugh at the sorrows he endured.

Rumi

We often suffer because we do not understand. Understanding is a great thing; once we understand, we can tolerate.

Inayat Khan

Asian Words of Inspiration

Non-cooperation with evil is as much a duty as is cooperation with good.

                        Mohandas Karamchand (Mahatma) Gandhi

The most secure place to hide a treasure of gold is in some desolate, unnoticed place. After all, why would anyone hide treasure in plain sight? And so it is said "Joy is hidden beneath sorrow."

                        Rumi

Let us rise up and be thankful, for if we didn't learn a lot today, at least we learned a little, and if we didn't learn a little, at least we didn't get sick, and if we got sick, at least we didn't die; so, let us be thankful.

                        Buddha

There is only one time when it is essential to awaken. That time is now.

                        Buddha

I have done my best. That is about all the philosophy of living one needs.

                        Lin Yutang

Asian Words of Inspiration

Whenever you take a step forward, you are bound to disturb something.

Indira Gandhi

A self-realized man remains happy without being affected by false appearances, whereas the ignorant man is miserable.

Sri Ramana Maharshi

Everything is meaningless, if you take it part by part. Everything is wonderful, if you take it as a whole. So, whatever you want to see, you must see as a whole structure.

Swami Krishnananda Saraswati

We can only win over the opponent by love, never by hate. Hate is the subtlest form of violence. We cannot be really non-violent and yet have hate in us.

Mohandas Karamchand (Mahatma) Gandhi

The man of understanding who has lost his identity as a separate individual remains identified with pure, infinite Consciousness while he continues to live out his life as an ordinary person in the world, knowing full well, however, that it is all an illusion.

Ramesh S. Balsekar

Asian Words of Inspiration

The sage is indifferent. He does not hanker after more pleasure, nor does he refuse whatever may come to him by way of experience. There is no volition, either positive or negative, because there is no separate entity to choose, want or strive for anything.

Ramesh S. Balsekar

It is only the body-mind apparatus that is involved in, or reacts to, any experience, and it can react only according to the way it is genetically made and shaped by past conditioning. Therefore, what is there to worry about or try to change? The one who understands Truth knows for a fact "I do nothing at all."

Ramesh S. Balsekar

You can chain me, you can torture me, you can even destroy this body, but you will never imprison my mind.

Mohandas Karamchand (Mahatma) Gandhi

All action is spontaneous, and all volition is an illusion. Once this is realized, one ceases to try to be spontaneous. Seeing the falseness of volition makes all action automatically spontaneous.

Ramesh S. Balsekar

Asian Words of Inspiration

It is health that is real wealth and not pieces of gold and silver.

Mohandas Karamchand (Mahatma) Gandhi

Wherever you stand, be the Soul of that place.

Rumi

There are four things which support the world:
1. The Learning of the Wise.
2. The Justice of the great.
3. The Prayer of the good.
4. The Valor of the brave.

Prophet Muhammad

In this world hate never yet dispelled hate. Only love dispels hate. This is the law, ancient and inexhaustible.

Buddha

What is the meaning of life? To be happy and useful.

The Dalai Lama

People take different roads seeking fulfillment and happiness. Just because they are not on your road doesn't mean they've gotten lost.

Dalai Lama

Asian Words of Inspiration

Morality is the attunement of oneself to the atmosphere one finds oneself in at any time. It is always changing with the evolutionary process to which the individual is subject. Morality is relative from place to place, time to time, but the necessity for morality is absolute.

Swami Krishnananda Saraswati

Every pleasure, physical or mental, needs an instrument. Both the physical and mental instruments are materials, they get tired and worn out. The pleasure they yield is necessarily limited in intensity and duration. Pain is the background of all your pleasures. You want them because you suffer. On the other hand, the very search for pleasure is the cause of pain. It is a vicious circle.

Nisargadatta Maharaj

Liberation is our very nature. We are that. The very fact that we wish for liberation shows that freedom from all bondage is our real nature. It is not to be freshly acquired. All that is necessary is to get rid of the false notion that we are bound. When we achieve that, there will be no desire or thought of any sort. So long as one desires liberation, so long, you may take it, one is in bondage.

Sri Ramana Maharshi

Asian Words of Inspiration

We are here to awaken from the illusion of our separateness.
                                              Thich Nhat Hanh

Those who cannot forgive others break the bridge over which they themselves must pass.
                                              Confucius

The resistance to the unpleasant situation is the root of suffering.
                                              Baba Ram Dass

Possession of material riches, without inner peace, is like dying of thirst while bathing in a lake.
                                              Paramahansa Yogananda

The heart is comforted by true words, just as a thirsty man is comforted by water.
                                              Rumi

Your work is to discover your world and then with all your heart give yourself to it.
                                              Buddha

God has no religion.
                    Mohandas Karamchand (Mahatma) Gandhi

Asian Words of Inspiration

When you are content to be simply yourself and don't compare or compete, everybody will respect you.

Lao-Tzu

Sincerity is the treasure of a land, for it is in sincerity that the people find their strength in times of hardship.

Confucius

It is vital that when educating our children's brains that we do not neglect to educate their hearts.

Dalai Lama

Life is really simple, but we insist on making it complicated.

Confucius

My experience is that everything is bliss. But the desire for bliss creates pain. Thus bliss becomes the seed of pain. The entire universe of pain is born of desire. Give up the desire for pleasure and you will not even know what is pain.

Nisargadatta Maharaj

If we call ourselves children of God, then others are also children of God.

Sri Chinmoy

Asian Words of Inspiration

If you light a lamp for someone else it will also brighten your path.

Buddha

What is birth and death but the beginning and the ending of a stream of events in consciousness? Because of the idea of separation and limitation they are painful. Momentary relief from pain we call pleasure, and we build castles in the air hoping for endless pleasure which we call happiness. It is all misunderstanding and misuse. Wake up, go beyond, live really.

Nisargadatta Maharaj

We are ultimately, in what we call a spiritual sense, neither human beings, nor males nor females, but only forces of Nature which have concentrated themselves in certain space-time points, looking like individuals. This is how self-analysis has to be carried on. When you think along these lines, you will find that your mind becomes "total" instead of fragmentary.

Swami Krishnananda Saraswati

What you now have is all you'll ever have.

Ram Tzu

Asian Words of Inspiration

Water doesn't lose purity because of a bit of weed. The weeds float on the surface; the pure water flows on undisturbed.

Rumi

Seekers continue to practice all kinds of self-torture without realizing that such 'spiritual practice' is a reinforcement of the very ego that keeps them from their natural, free state.

Ramesh S. Balsekar

Keep in tune with the source and all your actions will be correct. If you don't there will be trouble no matter what you do. With arrogance of ego there is not skillfulness and without arrogance everything is skillful.

Hariwansh Lal (Papaji) Poonja

Fiery lust is not diminished by indulging it, but inevitably by leaving it ungratified. As long as you are laying logs on the fire, the fire will burn. When you withhold the wood, the fire dies.

Rumi

All these griefs within our hearts arise from the smoke and dust of our existence and vain desires.

Rumi

Asian Words of Inspiration

There can be no technique or system for that total transformation in viewpoint called enlightenment for the simple reason that all effort must necessarily emanate from the illusory ego, that very mind of thought-intellect which has brought about the sorry plight from which the individual seeks freedom.

Ramesh S. Balsekar

Evil (ignorance) is like a shadow — it has no real substance of its own, it is simply a lack of light. You cannot cause a shadow to disappear by trying to fight it, stamp on it, by railing against it, or any other form of emotional or physical resistance. In order to cause a shadow to disappear, you must shine light on it.

Shakti Gawain

I have nothing new to teach the world. Truth and Non-violence are as old as the hills. All I have done is to try experiments in both on as vast a scale as I could.

Mohandas Karamchand (Mahatma) Gandhi

No matter how hard the past, you can always begin again.

Buddha

Asian Words of Inspiration

Pain and pleasure, good and bad, right and wrong; these are relative terms and must not be taken absolutely. They are limited and temporary.

Nisargadatta Maharaj

Essence is emptiness. Everything else, accidental. Emptiness brings peace to your loving. Everything else, disease. In this world of trickery emptiness is what your soul wants.

Rumi

Basic truth is non-denominational, non-dogmatic, universal.

Swami Amar Jyoti

Nothing can make you happier than you are. All search for happiness is misery and leads to more misery. The only happiness worth the name is the natural happiness of conscious being.

Nisargadatta Maharaj

The mind that projects the world, colors it its own way. When you meet a person, they are a stranger. When you marry them, they become your own self. When you quarrel, they become your enemy. It is your mind's attitude that determines what they are to you.

Nisargadatta Maharaj

Asian Words of Inspiration

At a time when opportunism is everything, when hope seems lost, when everything boils down to a cynical business deal, we must find the courage to dream. To reclaim romance. The romance of believing in justice, freedom, and dignity. For everybody.

Arundhati Roy

Wisdom tells me I am nothing. Love tells me I am everything. Between the two my life flows.

Nisargadatta Maharaj

Every moment I shape my destiny with a chisel I am a carpenter of my own soul.

Rumi

There is more to life than increasing its speed.

Mohandas Karamchand (Mahatma) Gandhi

New beginnings are often disguised as painful endings.

Lao-Tzu

If you correct your mind, the rest of your life will fall into place.

Lao-Tzu

Asian Words of Inspiration

What the caterpillar calls the end, the rest of the world calls a butterfly.

Lao-Tzu

Those who flow as life flows know they need no other force.

Lao-Tzu

Whatever purifies you is the correct road, I will not try to define it.

Rumi

Reality is simply the loss of ego. Destroy the ego by seeking its identity. Because the ego is no entity it will automatically vanish and reality will shine forth by itself.

Sri Ramana Maharshi

You seem to want instant insight, forgetting that the instant is always preceded by a long preparation. The fruit falls suddenly, but the ripening takes time.

Nisargadatta Maharaj

I find hope in the darkest of days, and focus in the brightest. I do not judge the universe.

Dalai Lama

Asian Words of Inspiration

The higher type of man clings to virtue, the lower type of man clings to material comfort. The higher type of man cherishes justice, the lower type of man cherishes the hope of favors to be received.

Confucius

When a baby is taken from the wet nurse, it easily forgets her and starts eating solid food. Seeds feed awhile on the ground, then lift up into the sun. So you should taste the filtered light and work your way toward wisdom with no personal covering. That's how you came here, like a star without a name. Move across the night sky with those anonymous lights.

Rumi

He who takes medicine and neglects to diet wastes the skills of his doctors.

Chinese Proverb

If you look deeply into the palm of your hand, you will see your parents and all generations of your ancestors. All of them are alive in this moment. Each is present in your body. You are the continuation of each of these people.

Thich Nhat Hanh

Asian Words of Inspiration

Children learn to smile from their parents.

           Shinichi Suzuki

In a gentle way, you can shake the world.

      Mohandas Karamchand (Mahatma) Gandhi

There is nothing that wastes the body like worry, and one who has any faith in God should be ashamed to worry about anything whatsoever.

      Mohandas Karamchand (Mahatma) Gandhi

A family is a place where minds come in contact with one another. If these minds love one another the home will be as beautiful as a flower garden. But if these minds get out of harmony with one another it is like a storm that plays havoc with the garden.

                Buddha

To support mother and father, to cherish wife and child and to have a simple livelihood; this is the good luck.

                Buddha

Nature does not hurry, yet everything is accomplished.

                Lao-Tzu

Asian Words of Inspiration

In dwelling, live close to the ground. In thinking, keep to the simple. In conflict, be fair and generous. In governing, don't try to control. In work, do what you enjoy. In family life, be completely present.

Lao-Tzu

We loosely talk of self-realization, for lack of a better term. But how can one real-ize or make real that which alone is real? All we need to do is to give up our habit of regarding as real that which is unreal. All religious practices are meant solely to help us do this. When we stop regarding the unreal as real, then reality alone will remain, and we will be that.

Sri Ramana Maharshi

I should love to satisfy all, if I possibly can; but in trying to satisfy all, I may be able to satisfy none. I have, therefore, arrived at the conclusion that the best course is to satisfy one's own conscience and leave the world to form its own judgment, favorable or otherwise.

Mohandas Karamchand (Mahatma) Gandhi

The man who embraces the world as real, like the man embracing a woman in his dream, ultimately awakens to find nothing there but himself.

Ramesh S. Balsekar

Asian Words of Inspiration

Forgiveness is the attribute of the strong.

     Mohandas Karamchand (Mahatma) Gandhi

A negative, pessimistic attitude of utter condemnation of the world is wrong. But excessive love, being captivated by the beauty of the world, is equally wrong. The truth is somewhere in the middle.

     Swami Krishnananda Saraswati

The desire for truth is the highest of all desires, yet it is still a desire. All desires must be given up for the real to be. Remember that you are. This is your working capital. Rotate it and there will be much profit.

     Nisargadatta Maharaj

Companionship with the holy makes you one of them. Though you are rock or marble, you'll become a jewel when you reach the man of heart.

     Rumi

It's dangerous to be something; it's foolish to be nothing; it's wise to be everything.

     Swami Amar Jyoti

Asian Words of Inspiration

Do not sit long with a sad friend. When you go to a garden, do you look at thorns or flowers? Spend more time with roses and jasmine.

Rumi

The only way that worry will stop is through the proper understanding that change is the very basis of life, that we cannot continuously have something we like. We're got to be prepared to accept things in life which may not be acceptable.

Ramesh S. Balsekar

Honesty is the gateway to success; it is indeed 50% of success. Learning is not necessary, no need to be learned. All that you have to do is to be sure and sincere that you are crying for (principle) only and nothing else. Let the aim of life be clear in your mind, first. I repeat, your aim should be nothing other than the Ultimate Reality.

Swami Krishnananda Saraswati

Why worry so much about causation? What do causes matter, when things themselves are transient? Let come what comes and let go what goes. Why catch hold of things and enquire about their causes?

Nisargadatta Maharaj

Asian Words of Inspiration

If the thought of sorrow spoils your joy, yet it prepares you for joy. Sorrow sweeps the house fiercely, emptying it of everything, then, coming from the Source of goodness, a new joy enters. Sorrow chases away the withered leaves in the heart, then new green leaves can grow. Sorrow uproots the previous joy, then a new delight springs from beyond.

Rumi

Be still like a mountain, and flow like a great river.

Lao-Tzu

As a breeze carries the Ocean inside it, so underneath every sentence is: "Come back to the Source."

Rumi

What you are is what you have been. What you will be is what you do now.

Buddha

Every human being's essential nature is perfect and faultless, but after years of immersion in the world we easily forget our roots and take on a counterfeit nature.

Lao-Tzu

Asian Words of Inspiration

There should be balance in all our actions; to be either extreme or lukewarm is equally bad.

Inayat Khan

I have just three things to teach: simplicity, patience, compassion. These three are your greatest treasures.

Lao-Tzu

Whatever happens in the working of the universe at the present moment has to be accepted. Not accepting it means human misery.

Ramesh S. Balsekar

Thousands of candles can be lighted from a single candle, and the life of the candle will not be shortened. Happiness never decreases by being shared.

Buddha

The secret to bliss is to stop the search, stop thinking, stop not-thinking, and keep quiet. The best practice is to know "Who am I." You are Brahman, know this.

Hariwansh Lal (Papaji) Poonja

Asian Words of Inspiration

When you see a pearl on the bottom, you reach through the foam and broken sticks on the surface. When the sun comes up, you forget about locating the constellation of Scorpio. When you see the splendor of union, the attractions of duality seem poignant and lovely, but much less interesting.

Rumi

Be vigilant of the present circumstances. This is quite enough to give you happiness. Be vigilant only of this moment! When this happening goes, don't cling to it. Clinging to past circumstances is the trouble with everybody. This is the cause of suffering and misery. What has happened cannot be brought back, so it is reasonable to not cling to it. Simply do not cling to past circumstances. Don't cling to the past.

Hariwansh Lal (Papaji) Poonja

At the intellectual level there can be no end to questions. Instead, hang on to the one who is asking. That is all you need do. Indeed, there is nothing else really that you could do. If you can do this, never allowing the self to escape your attention, you will ultimately find that the seeker is none other than consciousness seeking its own source and that the seeker himself is both the seeking and the sought, and THAT IS YOU.

Ramesh S. Balsekar

Asian Words of Inspiration

Life can be really and truly simple if we don't fight it.

> Ramesh S. Balsekar

If you look to others for fulfillment, you will never truly be fulfilled.

> Lao-Tzu

The enemy is fear. We think it is hate, but it is fear.

> Mohandas Karamchand (Mahatma) Gandhi

Claim wealth and titles, and disaster will follow.

> Lao-Tzu

Enlightenment is intimacy with all things.

> Dōgen Zenji

All thoughts and emotions are not real. They are like the waves that dance on the surface of the ocean for a few seconds or minutes and then they return to where they have arisen from. Then they are no more wave, but they are ocean. How long can a wave keep its form as a separate personality?

> Hariwansh Lal (Papaji) Poonja

Asian Words of Inspiration

I see the same world as you do, but not the same way. There is nothing mysterious about it. Everybody sees the world through the idea he has of himself. As you think yourself to be, so you think the world to be. If you imagine yourself as separate from the world, the world will appear as separate from you and you will experience desire and fear. I do not see the world as separate from me and so there is nothing for me to desire, or fear.

Nisargadatta Maharaj

Do you think you can take over the universe and improve it? I do not believe it can be done. The universe is sacred. You cannot improve it. If you try to change it, you will ruin it. If you try to hold it, you will lose it. So sometimes things are ahead and sometimes they are behind; Sometimes breathing is hard, sometimes it comes easily; Sometimes there is strength and sometimes weakness; Sometimes one is up and sometimes down. Therefore the sage avoids extremes, excesses, and complacency.

Lao-Tzu

Trying to control the mind forcefully is like trying to flatten out waves with a board. It can only result in further disturbance.

Ramesh S. Balsekar

Asian Words of Inspiration

What you seek is pleasure and not an object. So do not make the mistake of thinking that your mind wants this or that object. You do not want anything, only pleasure. And if you think that a particular object can give pleasure you go near it, but if it does not give satisfaction you will leave it alone and go to another place for another object. In this way, your life is spent looking for pleasure and not for a particular object which it really cannot find. And nowhere will you find this pleasure you are seeking — nowhere — because it is not a commodity of this world. It belongs to some other realm altogether.

Swami Krishnananda Saraswati

Holding on to anger is like grasping a hot coal with the intent of throwing it at someone else; you are the one who gets burned.

Chinese Proverb

No one ever won a chess game by betting on each move. Sometimes you have to move backward to get a step forward.

Amar Gopal Bose

Nothing coming, nothing owed.

Lalla

Asian Words of Inspiration

True friends want nothing from you except the joy of your presence. No matter what you do, they will always be your friend.

                                        Paramahansa Yogananda

Human beings actually have no more independence or autonomy in living their lives than do the characters in a dream. Neither do they have anything to do with the creation of the dream or anything in it. They are simply being lived along with everything else in this living dream of the manifested universe. The entire dream is unreal. Only the dreamer is real, and that is Consciousness itself.

                                        Ramesh S. Balsekar

Hatred and fear blind us. We no longer see each other. We see only the faces of monsters, and that gives us the courage to destroy each other.

                                        Thich Nhat Hanh

Self is always Present, Bliss is always Present. You are not to work at attaining it, just remove the obstacles by which you can't see it. The hindrance is only one: Attachment to the past.

                              Hariwansh Lal (Papaji) Poonja

Asian Words of Inspiration

Children are living beings — more living than grown-up people who have built shells of habit around themselves. Therefore it is absolutely necessary for their mental health and development that they should not have mere schools for their lessons, but a world whose guiding spirit is personal love.

Rabindranath Tagore

Don't search for it. It is nothing, and a nothing within nothing.

Lalla

Feed your heart in conversation with someone harmonious with it; seek spiritual advancement from one who is advanced.

Rumi

To decrease thought is to increase spirit. To decrease over-exertion is to increase strength. To decrease words is to foster vital energy.

Awa Kenzo
Zen Bow, Zen Arrow

Speak honestly or else be silent.

Rumi

Asian Words of Inspiration

Heaven and earth are impartial; they see the ten thousand things as straw dogs. The wise are impartial; they see the people as straw dogs.

Lao-Tzu

The world's flattery and hypocrisy is a sweet morsel: eat less of it, for it is full of fire. Its fire is hidden while its taste is manifest, but its smoke becomes visible in the end.

Rumi

If some Power has turned you into a seeker, don't you think it is the responsibility of that Power to take you where you are supposed to be taken?

Ramesh S. Balsekar

To exist means to be something, a thing, feeling, thought, idea. All existence is particular. Only being is universal, in the sense that every being is compatible with every other being. Existences clash, being — never. Existence means becoming: change, birth and death and birth again, while in being there is silent peace.

Nisargadatta Maharaj

Asian Words of Inspiration

Time, the fear of the unknown, and thought which projects what it wants for tomorrow are all bound together in one package that spells conflict, separation, and misery.

Ramesh S. Balsekar

A newborn baby is the purest form of a human being. This purity remains until the baby understands my/mine, you/yours.

Baba Hari Dass

We take long trips. We puzzle over the meaning of a painting or a book, when what we're wanting to see and understand in this world, we are that.

Rumi

All the powers in the universe are already ours. It is we who have put our hands before our eyes and cry that it is dark. Know that there is no darkness around us. Take the hands away and there is the light, which was from the beginning. Darkness never existed, weakness never existed. We who are fools cry that we are weak; we who are fools cry that we are impure. Thus Vedanta not only insists that the ideal is practical, but that it has been so all the time, and this ideal, this Reality is our own nature.

Swami Vivekananda

Asian Words of Inspiration

People become speechless at the sight of the trees, the flowers, the pond. But, alas, how few are they who seek the owner of all these?

Ramakrishna Paramahamsa

Following enlightenment, you want to practice more and more.

Awa Kenzo
Zen Bow, Zen Arrow

For every force there is a counterforce. Violence, even well intentioned, always rebounds upon itself.

Lao-Tzu

The Tao that can be told is not the eternal Tao.
The name that can be named is not the eternal name.
The nameless is the beginning of heaven and earth.
The named is the mother of ten thousand things.
Ever desireless, one can see the mystery.
Ever desiring, one sees the manifestations.
These two spring from the same source but differ in name; this appears as darkness.
Darkness within darkness.
The gate to all mystery.

Lao-Tzu

Asian Words of Inspiration

If you're respectful by habit, constantly honoring the worthy, four things increase: long life, beauty, happiness, strength.

Buddha

Every human being is the author of his own health and disease.

Buddha

Health is the greatest gift, contentment the greatest wealth, faithfulness the best relationship.

Buddha

There is force in the Universe, which, if we permit it, will flow through us and produce miraculous results.

Mohandas Karamchand (Mahatma) Gandhi

We need to be aware of the suffering, but retain our clarity, calmness, and strength so we can help transform the situation.

Thich Nhat Hanh

Someone who goes home with half a loaf of bread to a small place that fits like a nest around him, someone who wants no more, who is not longed for by anyone else, he's a letter to everyone. You open it. It says "Live!"

Rumi

Asian Words of Inspiration

The very idea of going beyond the dream is illusory. Why go anywhere? Just realize that you are dreaming a dream you call the world, and stop looking for ways out. The dream is not your problem. Your problem is that you like one part of your dream and not another. Love all, or none of it, and stop complaining. When you have seen the dream as a dream, you have done all that need be done.

Nisargadatta Maharaj

We have a largely materialistic lifestyle characterized by a materialistic culture. However, this only provides us with temporary, sensory satisfaction, whereas long-term satisfaction is based not on the senses but on the mind. That's where real tranquility is to be found. And peace of mind turns out to be a significant factor in our physical health too.

Dalai Lama

Be careful what you choose to do consciously, for unless your will is very strong, that is what you may have to do repeatedly and compulsively through the habit-influencing power of the subconscious mind.

Paramahansa Yogananda

Asian Words of Inspiration

The present difficulty is that man thinks he is the doer. But it man is only a tool. If he accepts that position he is free from troubles, otherwise he courts them.

Sri Ramana Maharshi

To each person that way is the best which appears easiest or appeals most. All the ways are equally good, as they lead to the same goal, which is the merging of the ego with the Self. What the *bhakta* (devotee) calls surrender, the man who does *vichara* calls *jnana*. Both are trying to take the ego back to the source from which it sprang and make it merge there.

Sri Ramana Maharshi

People have a hard time letting go of their suffering. Out of a fear of the unknown, they prefer suffering that is familiar.

Thich Nhat Hanh

Freedom is not worth having if it does not connote freedom to err. It passes my comprehension how human beings, be they ever so experienced and able, can delight in depriving other human beings of that precious right.

Mohandas Karamchand (Mahatma) Gandhi

Wishes may or may not come true in this house of disappointment. Let's push the door open together and leave.

Rumi

Asian Words of Inspiration

One of the signs of God-realization is joy. There is absolutely no hesitancy in such a person, who is like an ocean in joyous waves. But deep beneath the surface, there is profound silence and peace.

Ramakrishna Paramahamsa

If consciousness is paired with another consciousness, light increases and the way becomes clear; but if a beast joins with another, darkness increases and the way disappears.

Rumi

You do not come from somewhere, you do not go anywhere. You are timeless being and awareness.

Nisargadatta Maharaj

Freedom is not given to us by anyone; we have to cultivate it ourselves. It is a daily practice.

Thich Nhat Hanh

When you desire the common good, the whole world desires with you. Make humanity's desire your own and work for it. There you cannot fail.

Nisargadatta Maharaj

Asian Words of Inspiration

No object of desire is real. No object of desire is worth your peace. If your house is desires, burn it down. It is only the absence of desire that makes you happy, so allow no desire to rise. Just allow yourself to be dissolved by love. When there is no desire there is love and beauty. If you do desire then only desire peace because what you think you will become. Water poured in the ocean becomes the ocean.

Hariwansh Lal (Papaji) Poonja

If you know you are bound you are no longer bound because by knowing the bondage you separate yourself from it, you objectify it. With this release the "I" that was bound pours into Consciousness like a river pours into the Ocean.

Hariwansh Lal (Papaji) Poonja

Your world is transient, changeful. My world is perfect, changeless. You can tell me what you like about your world — I shall listen carefully, even with interest, yet not for a moment shall I forget that your world is not, that you are dreaming.

Nisargadatta Maharaj

Happiness is your nature. It is not wrong to desire it. What is wrong is seeking it outside when it is inside.

Sri Ramana Maharshi

Asian Words of Inspiration

Seeing truly is not merely a change in the direction of seeing but a change in its very center, in which the seer himself disappears.

Ramesh S. Balsekar

To the extent that an individual wishes to experience the world as separate from himself, he is a spectacle without a spectator. To the extent that he prefers to be insensitive to the world, he is a spectator without a spectacle. But it is only when life is accepted totally, however it comes, knowing it to be nothing but a dream yet acting intuitively as if it is real, that one will experience life fully as the natural spectator of the natural spectacle.

Ramesh S. Balsekar

The further one goes, the more difficulties there are. One finds greater faults in oneself as one advances along the spiritual path. It is not because the number of faults has increased, but the sense has become so keen that one regards differently faults that formerly one would not have noticed. It is like a musician: the more he advances and the better he plays, the more faults he notices. He who does not notice his faults is in reality becoming worse. There is no end to one's faults. To think of them makes one humble.

Inayat Khan

Asian Words of Inspiration

The Supreme is the universal solvent, it corrodes every container, it burns through every obstacle. Without the absolute denial of everything the tyranny of things would be absolute. The Supreme is the great harmonizer, the guarantee of the ultimate and perfect balance — of life in freedom. It dissolves you and thus re-asserts your true being.

Nisargadatta Maharaj

Between the banks of pain and pleasure, the river of life flows. It is only when the mind refuses to flow with life, and gets stuck at the banks, that it becomes a problem. By flowing with life, I mean acceptance — letting come what comes and go what goes. Desire not, fear not, observe the actual, as and when it happens, for you are not what happens, you are to whom it happens. Ultimately even the observer you are not.

Nisargadatta Maharaj

The only condition for the realization of Truth is that the knowledge of it be desired with tremendous intensity. You cannot see it, you cannot feel it only because you do not really want it — you are too preoccupied with enjoying and sorrowing over your finite existence.

Ramesh S. Balsekar

Asian Words of Inspiration

Develop the witness attitude and you will find in your own experience that detachment brings control. The state of witnessing is full of power, there is nothing passive about it.

Nisargadatta Maharaj

Everything has its place in the world as well as in our daily routine. Devotion and reverence are all right, for example, so long as one recognizes them for what they are —affectivity— and to that extent a form of bondage. When one sees something for what it is, it then loses its force and cannot effect any further bondage.

Ramesh S. Balsekar

In a true non-objective relationship we do not love others, we ARE others.

Ramesh S. Balsekar

Reality divided by reason always leaves a remainder.

Haridas Chaudhuri

When you make a choice, you change the future.

Deepak Chopra

Asian Words of Inspiration

These forms are transient and to be attached to them is to be confused. Anything that rises, be it thought, desire, emotion, feeling, or object will give you suffering and no one in the world can avoid this. Both the enjoyer and the enjoyed are washed away. But the wise discriminate between the Real and the unreal. They know what is Real and so allow their feelings and thoughts to arise because they know all is One and the same! In this way you will not suffer.

Hariwansh Lal (Papaji) Poonja

This world is really a long, long, dream. The five senses delude you at every moment. Open your eyes. Learn to discriminate. Understand His mysteries. Feel His presence everywhere, as well as His nearness. Believe me, He dwells in the chambers of your own heart. He is the silent witness of your mind. He is the holder of the string of your *prana*. He is the womb for this world and the Vedas. He is the prompter of thoughts. Search for Him inside your heart and obtain His grace. Then alone you have lived your life well.

Swami Sivananda

Silence is the ocean in which all the rivers of all the religions discharge themselves and lose their identity.

Sri Ramana Maharshi

Asian Words of Inspiration

There is the eye of the Sea and there is the foam. Leave the foam behind and look with the eye of the Sea. Day and night foam is born out of the Sea: how strange! You keep looking at the foam and not at the Sea!

Rumi

If your knowledge of fire has been turned to certainty by words alone, then seek to be cooked by the fire itself. Don't abide in borrowed certainty. There is no real certainty until you burn; if you wish for this, sit down in the fire.

Rumi

You are not in the body. The body is in you.

Nisargadatta Maharaj

Letting go gives us freedom and freedom is the only condition for happiness.

Thich Nhat Hanh

A good traveler has no fixed plans, and is not intent on arriving.

Lao-Tzu

The very center of your heart is where life begins — the most beautiful place on earth.

Rumi

Asian Words of Inspiration

You are searching for something without understanding that it is within you. Search within. This is a direct approach. Do not search for God outside. God is already within you. When you come to know that God dwells within you, then your life will totally change and you will be transformed. When you have perfect control over the modifications of the mind, you will attain the highest level of consciousness or *samadhi*.

Swami Rama

I promise myself that I will enjoy every minute of the day that is given me to live.

Thich Nhat Hanh

The world belongs to humanity, not this leader, that leader, kings, or religious leaders. The world belongs to humanity. Each country belongs essentially to their own people.

Dalai Lama

There is no key to happiness. The door is always open.

Mother Teresa

Why are you so enchanted by this world, when a mine of gold lies within you?

Rumi

Asian Words of Inspiration

By God, when you see your beauty you'll be the idol of yourself.

                                                         Rumi

Don't move the way fear makes you move. Move the way love makes you move. Move the way joy makes you move.

                                                         Osho

No one saves us but ourselves. No one can and no one may. We ourselves must walk the path.

                                                       Buddha

If you conduct your life on the basis of truth and honesty, it gives you a sense of satisfaction and self-confidence.

                                               Dalai Lama

I would rather die a meaningful death than to live a meaningless life.

                                        Corazon Aquino

To be wronged is nothing unless you continue to remember it.

                                                Confucius

Asian Words of Inspiration

The role of destiny unfolds itself and actualizes the inevitable. You cannot change the course of events, but you can change your attitude and what really matters is the attitude and not the bare event.

Nisargadatta Maharaj

Whatever comes, let it come, what stays let stay, what goes let go — always keep quiet. The way to live a happy beautiful life is to accept whatever comes and not care about what does not come.

Hariwansh Lal (Papaji) Poonja

If one speaks or acts with a pure mind, happiness follows like a shadow.

Buddha

To straighten the crooked you must first do a harder thing; straighten yourself.

The Dhammapada

You are beyond happiness itself. You are that place where the waves of happiness arise from. Find that place, don't understand it. You have to simply see that you are That itself.

Hariwansh Lal (Papaji) Poonja

Asian Words of Inspiration

I have just three things to teach: simplicity, patience, compassion. These three are the greatest treasures. Simple in actions and thoughts, you return to the source of being. Patient with both friends and enemies, you accord with the way things are. Compassionate toward yourself, you reconcile all beings in the world.

Lao-Tzu

The best athlete wants his opponent at his best. The best general enters the mind of his enemy. All of them embody the virtue of non-competition. Not that they don't love to compete, but they do it in the spirit of play.

Lao-Tzu

The Noble Eightfold Path: Right view. Right thinking. Right speech. Right action. Right livelihood. Right effort. Right mindfulness. Right concentration.

Buddha

Less and less do you need to force things, until finally you arrive at non-action. When nothing is done, nothing is left undone.

Lao-Tzu

Asian Words of Inspiration

Old friends pass away, new friends appear. It is just like the days. An old day passes, a new day arrives. The important thing is to make it meaningful: a meaningful friend or a meaningful day.

Dalai Lama

To give pleasure to a single heart by a single act is better than a thousand heads bowing in prayer.

Mohandas Karamchand (Mahatma) Gandhi

Be aware of being conscious and seek the source of consciousness. That is all. Very little can be conveyed in words. It is the doing as I tell you that will bring light, not my telling you. The means do not matter much; it is the desire, the urge, the earnestness that counts.

Nisargadatta Maharaj

Blessed is he who makes his companions laugh.

The Koran

The soul has been given its own ears to hear things mind does not understand.

Rumi

Asian Words of Inspiration

All other knowledges are only petty and trivial knowledges; the experience of silence alone is the real and perfect knowledge. Know that the many objective differences are not real but are mere superimpositions on Self, which is the form of true knowledge.

Sri Ramana Maharshi

True understanding, which is enlightenment, can happen only when there is total effortlessness — in other words, in the utter absence of any comprehender. Then there is only the witnessing of the dream of life without the least desire to change anything.

Ramesh S. Balsekar

Raise your words, not your voice. It is rain that grows flowers, not thunder.

Rumi

The more light you allow within you, the brighter the world you live in will be.

Shakti Gawain

If one desires to receive one must first give. This is called profound understanding.

Lao-Tzu

Asian Words of Inspiration

Manifest plainness. Embrace simplicity. Reduce selfishness. Have few desires.

Lao-Tzu

For every hundred men hacking away at the branches of a diseased tree, only one will stoop to inspect the roots.

Chinese Proverb

We need to be aware of the suffering, but retain our clarity, calmness, and strength so we can help transform the situation.

Thich Nhat Hanh

He who smiles rather than rages is always the stronger.

Japanese Proverb

The fundamental and unchangeable fact is that there is no human being who can perform any act on his own, any more than can a puppet on strings.

Ramesh S. Balsekar

Being empty of desire is happiness. Return to your own Source and you are happy. This is the trick of happiness.

Hariwansh Lal (Papaji) Poonja

Asian Words of Inspiration

Why is the sea king of a hundred streams? Because it lies below them. Therefore it is the king of a hundred streams. If the sage would guide the people, he must serve with humility. If he would lead them, he must follow behind. In this way when the sage rules, the people will not feel oppressed. When he stands before them, they will not be harmed. The whole world will support him and will not tire of him. Because he does not compete, he does not meet competition.

Lao-Tzu

Freedom from all desire is eternity. All attachment implies fear, for all things are transient. And fear makes one a slave. This freedom from attachment does not come with practice; it is natural, when one knows one's true being. Love does not cling; clinging is not love.

Nisargadatta Maharaj

Men and women are beautiful masks. Behind them all is the same Divine Power who rises up gently through the six subtle centers of this human body, giving each person a unique flavor and intensity, unveiling through each living being a unique degree of Divine Manifestation.

Ramakrishna Paramahamsa

Asian Words of Inspiration

The Source supplies you with the energy to reach it. When you seek the Light, it shall enlighten your path. And when you are longing for the Divine, for the Truth, that shall give you power and energy to tread on.

Swami Amar Jyoti

The man of wisdom is devoid of ego even though he may appear to use it. His vacant or fasting mind is neither doing anything nor not doing anything. He is outside of volition, neither this nor that. He is everything and nothing.

Ramesh S. Balsekar

When man accepts finally that he cannot make sense out of life on the basis of anything fixed, then and only then can life make sense.

Ramesh S. Balsekar

The Great Way is not difficult for those who have no preferences. When love and hate are both absent everything becomes clear and undisguised. Make the smallest distinction, however, and heaven and earth are set infinitely apart.

Seng-Ts'an

Asian Words of Inspiration

Belief, any belief, is based on the sense of insecurity. Only when all belief is given up are you free to know yourself. In self-discovery what you find is the Truth — that Truth that is total, self-evident and that needs no outside support or justification.

Ramesh S. Balsekar

Forgetting that Being you are lost into the process of becoming. You get tied up with becoming something all the time you want to be this, you want to be that. You don't want to end the becoming into Being wherein lies the whole secret of becoming. Becoming is itself not an independent something, it's a radiation of Being, a projection of Consciousness, that basic eternal Essence which Thou art.

Swami Amar Jyoti

Still your mind in me, still yourself in me, and without a doubt you shall be united with me, Lord of Love, dwelling in your heart.

Bhagavad Gita

There is no path to happiness; happiness is the path.

Buddha

Asian Words of Inspiration

Do what you feel like doing. Don't bully yourself. Violence will make you hard and rigid. Do not fight with what you take to be obstacles in your way. Just be interested in them, watch them, observe, enquire. Let anything happen — good or bad. But don't let yourself be submerged by what happens.

                                                Nisargadatta Maharaj

Besides the noble art of getting things done, there is the noble art of leaving things undone. The wisdom of life consists in the elimination of non-essentials.

                                                Lin Yutang

You must not lose faith in humanity. Humanity is like an ocean; if a few drops of the ocean are dirty, the ocean does not become dirty.

                          Mohandas Karamchand (Mahatma) Gandhi

He who knows that enough is enough will always have enough.

                                                  Lao-Tzu

People's memories are maybe the fuel they burn to stay alive.

                                                Haruki Murakami

Asian Words of Inspiration

The mystic dances in the sun, hearing music others don't. "Insanity," they say. If so, it's a very gentle, nourishing sort.

Rumi

People usually consider walking on water or in thin air a miracle but I think the real miracle is not to walk either on water or in thin air, but to walk on earth. Every day we are engaged in a miracle which we don't even recognize: a blue sky, white clouds, green leaves, the black, curious eyes of a child — our own two eyes. All is a miracle.

Thich Nhat Han

In the attitude of silence the soul finds the path in a clearer light and what is elusive and deceptive resolves itself into crystal clearness. Our life is a long and arduous quest after Truth.

Mohandas Karamchand (Mahatma) Gandhi

Once the mirror of your heart is clear and pure, you will see images beyond this world of water and clay. You will see both the image and the maker of images, both the carpet of the kingdom and him who lays the carpet.

Rumi

Asian Words of Inspiration

"Truth shall make you free." That's crisp, crystal clear. It can survive any argument, discussion or debate. Truth can stand any challenges, not by its own determination but by its own proven victory; not by what I say or you say, but by Itself, Truth shines. It shall prevail.

Swami Amar Jyoti

To any conceptual problem there cannot be any valid answer except to see the problem in perspective as an empty thought. There is no such things as a "problem" which is other than merely conceptual.

Ramesh S. Balsekar

To divide and particularize is in the mind's very nature. There is no harm in dividing. But separation goes against fact. Things and people are different, but they are not separate. Nature is one, reality is one. There are opposites, but no opposition.

Nisargadatta Maharaj

If changes are necessary, they will happen. And if something changes — you do something new or you cease doing something — there's no need to feel any guilt. It's part of the functioning of Totality.

Ramesh S. Balsekar

Asian Words of Inspiration

Forge your spirit through actual practice and experience. Your spirit is not your slave. It needs nourishment.

Awa Kenzo

Zen Bow, Zen Arrow

How you do one thing is how you do everything.

Zen Proverb

A child without education is like a bird without wings.

Tibetan Proverb

You are the garden of joy, to be happy you need nobody else. You are in the garden of joy, but when you think of old things, you become sad. This joy, this moment, will destroy suffering, because this moment is happiness. So stop going to the past moments in order to suffer.

Hariwansh Lal (Papaji) Poonja

How many victories are won without spiritual struggle and patience? To show patience for the sake of the cup of Divine Knowledge is no hardship. Show patience, for patience is the key to joy.

Rumi

Asian Words of Inspiration

Man frees himself from the world, its ills, its suffering, and its chaos simply by seeing the absurdity of it all.

              Ramesh S. Balsekar

The further you go, the less you know. The sage knows without traveling; sees without looking; works without doing.

                     Lao-Tzu

The trouble is, you think you have time.

                     Buddha

True happiness cannot arise until the identification with the body-mind apparatus is demolished.

              Ramesh S. Balsekar

The person who removes a mountain begins by carrying away small stones.

                Chinese Proverb

The body is a material thing and needs time to change. The mind is but a set of mental habits, of ways of thinking and feeling, and to change they must be brought to the surface and examined. This also takes time. Just resolve and persevere, the rest will take care of itself.

              Nisargadatta Maharaj

Asian Words of Inspiration

If you want it (realization), it will come. There is no qualification necessary, except wanting it. That is the only qualification. If it is not wanted, it will not come. It comes when it is wanted, but wanted wholly, not a little.

Swami Krishnananda Saraswati

Fortunate is he who does not walk with envy as his companion.

Rumi

The thought of God is like a fire that will burn all desires. The highest knowledge is nothing but the deep feeling of the presence of God everywhere. That is the highest wisdom and that will give a death-blow to other desires of the world. The desire for God is a desire to destroy all desires.

Swami Krishnananda Saraswati

Surrender is to surrender your concept of separateness, your ego. Surrender is to submit your stupidness, your wickedness, to the will of Existence. That's all. You must surrender like a river discharging into the Ocean. Surrender is to discharge your river of separateness into the Ocean of Being, losing your limitations and allowing to happen what happens.

Hariwansh Lal (Papaji) Poonja

Asian Words of Inspiration

Faith is a great wealth and gives you strength. Just because a few small things did not go in your favor, it does not mean that you should make your faith so fragile and delicate that it breaks every now and then.

Sri Sri Ravi Shankar

The sparrow is sorry for the peacock at the burden of his tail.

Rabindranath Tagore

The Teacher is one who knows the Truth and can transmit this Truth to a humble one by look, by touch, by thought, or as Arunachala does, by Silence. This Silence is the Light that does not move.

Hariwansh Lal (Papaji) Poonja

Every child's life is like a piece of paper on which every person leaves a mark.

Chinese Proverb

Recompense injury with justice, recompense kindness with kindness.

Confucius

Asian Words of Inspiration

When the country is ruled with a light hand the people are simple. When the country is ruled with severity, the people are cunning.

Lao-Tzu

The more awake one is to the material world, the more one is asleep to spirit.

Rumi

What the world wants is character.

Swami Vivekananda

Live as if you were to die tomorrow. Learn as if you were to live forever.

Mohandas Karamchand (Mahatma) Gandhi

If you but cease from useless conceptualizing, you will be what you are and what you have always been.

Ramesh S. Balsekar

Those who say it cannot be done, should not interrupt those doing it.

Chinese Proverb

If you chase two rabbits, both will escape.

Chinese Proverb

Asian Words of Inspiration

As long as traces of hatred and anger are in you, you will not be able to find true peace. When you are finally able to love your enemy, you may feel like a great hero, but then you will see that, in truth, to love that person is to love your own self. When you open your heart and accept the person you once hated, quite naturally your heart will experience ease and you will be the first to receive the benefits. This is the true meaning of equanimity — equality without discrimination or prejudice.

Thich Nhat Hanh

First they ignore you, then they ridicule you, then they fight you, and then you win.

Mohandas Karamchand (Mahatma) Gandhi

Asian Words of Inspiration

Asian Words of Inspiration

Attaining Personal Goals

The best definition of success, in my opinion, comes from legendary UCLA basketball coach John Wooden, *"Success is peace of mind which is a direct result of self-satisfaction in knowing you did your best to become the best that you are capable of becoming."*

And in reality, this what all personal goals really aim to achieve — help each of us get closer to the best we are capable of.

Doing so takes commitment, dedication, courage, persistence, self-motivation, and focus. It also takes a willingness to try new things, learn from failure and setbacks, and have a consistent belief in yourself. Which is exactly what Asia's leading thinkers have been telling us for centuries!

Every one of us has options about what we will do with our lives and what we will make of ourselves. However, no matter what paths we choose and what options we select, once those decisions are made we basically have two choices:

Asian Words of Inspiration

   a) to be less than what we have the capacity to become, or

   b) to be all that we can be, to strive as best we can with the skills we have and under the circumstances given.

Here's a suggestion for you. Before you read the quotations and thoughts in this section, write down your top 10 personal goals for the next one to three years. Then, reflect on each quote to see how it might help you in pursuing your goals. At the end of this section, review your list and see if you want to amend, change, or add anything to your goals list.

And remember, again in the words of Coach Wooden: *"Do not let what you cannot do interfere with what you can do."*

Do not be vague. Make your intentions as clear as a bell. Praise others for their sincere words.

Awa Kenzo
Zen Bow, Zen Arrow

To be idle is a short road to death and to be diligent is a way of life; foolish people are idle, wise people are diligent.

Buddha

Asian Words of Inspiration

Being happy is of the utmost importance. Success in anything is through happiness. Under all circumstances be happy. Just think of any negativity that comes at you as a raindrop falling into the ocean of your bliss.

Maharishi Mahesh Yogi

It is useless to search for the truth, when the mind is blind to the false. It must be purged of the false completely before truth can dawn on it.

Nisargadatta Maharaj

Seeing the small is insight, yielding to force is strength. Using the outer light, return to insight, and in this way be saved from harm. This is learning constancy.

Lao-Tzu

Whatever may be the desire or fear, don't dwell upon it. Try and see for yourself. Here and there you may forget, it does not matter. Go back to your attempts till the brushing away of every desire and fear, of every reaction, becomes automatic.

Nisargadatta Maharaj

Asian Words of Inspiration

Success should be measured by the yardstick of happiness; by your ability to remain in peaceful harmony with cosmic laws.

Paramahansa Yogananda

Don't be a drop, become an ocean. If you want to be a sea, destroy the drop.

Rumi

It is very important to generate a good attitude, a good heart, as much as possible. From this, happiness in both the short term and the long term for both yourself and others will come.

Dalai Lama

In all things success depends on previous preparation, and without such previous preparation there is sure to be failure. If what is to be spoken be previously determined, there will be no stumbling. If affairs be previously determined, there will be no difficulty with them. If one's actions have been previously determined, there will be no sorrow in connection with them. If principles of conduct have been previously determined, the practice of them will be inexhaustible.

Confucius

Asian Words of Inspiration

Devotion without understanding is only emotion and later becomes a passion: fanaticism.
Swami Krishnananda Saraswati

If you enjoy what you do, you'll never work another day in your life.
Confucius

In the dojo, aim for truth.
At home, aim for harmony.
At work, aim for progress.
Among friends, aim for trust.
In the world, aim for sincerity.
Awa Kenzo
Zen Bow, Zen Arrow

Failure is due to lack of steadfastness. Steadfastness develops willpower. It helps quick growth and rapid evolution, and removes the stumbling blocks on the path of realization.
Swami Sivananda

One day of effort is one day of bliss; One day of sloth is a hundred years of regret.
Awa Kenzo
Zen Bow, Zen Arrow

Asian Words of Inspiration

We can solve many problems in an appropriate way, without any difficulty, if we cultivate harmony, friendship, and respect for one another.

Dalai Lama

The greatest Guru is your inner self. Truly, he is the supreme teacher. He alone can take you to your goal and he alone meets you at the end of the road. Confide in him and you need no outer Guru. But again you must have the strong desire to find him and do nothing that will create obstacles and delays. And do not waste energy and time on regrets. Learn from your mistakes and do not repeat them.

Nisargadatta Maharaj

It is very important to generate a good attitude, a good heart, as much as possible. From this, happiness in both the short term and the long term for both yourself and others will come.

Dalai Lama

The power of God is within you, so when your mind tells you a thing can't be done, say to that thought: get out! It can be done. And it will be, if you make up your mind.

Paramahansa Yogananda

Asian Words of Inspiration

Practice non-action. Work without doing. Taste the tasteless. Magnify the small, increase the few. Reward bitterness with care. See simplicity in the complicated. Achieve greatness in little things. In the universe the difficult things are done as if they are easy. In the universe great acts are made up of small deeds. The sage does not attempt anything very big, and thus achieves greatness. Easy promises make for little trust. Taking things lightly results in great difficulty. Because the sage always confronts difficulties, he never experiences them.

Lao-Tzu

Be in the company of people who think alike, not in that of people who think the opposite way. Be in an atmosphere holy and sacred; and to the extent possible, from your own point of view, have friends of this nature. Either have good friends or no friends but don't have bad friends. Bad friends will distract your mind and shake your faith by saying things contrary and illogical.

Swami Krishnananda Saraswati

I will not consider the faults of others or what they have or have not done. Rather, I will consider what I myself have done or have not done.

Buddha

Asian Words of Inspiration

Winners compare their achievements with their goals, while losers compare their achievements with those of other people.

              Nido Qubein

Always aim at complete harmony of thought and word and deed. Always aim at purifying your thoughts and everything will be well.

        Mohandas Karamchand (Mahatma) Gandhi

When you are inspired by some great purpose, some extraordinary project, all of your thoughts break their bonds. Your mind transcends limitations; your consciousness expands in every direction; and you find yourself in a new, great and wonderful world. Dormant forces, faculties, and talents become alive and you discover yourself to be a greater person than you ever dreamed yourself to be.

              Patañjali

However many holy words you read, however many you speak, what good will they do you if you do not act on upon them?

                Buddha

Asian Words of Inspiration

All you can do is act your role to the best of your ability. The consequences are not in your hands.

> Ramesh S. Balsekar

Desire excites. Excitement may sometimes elevate us but will depress us eventually. Inspiration elevates further and further.

> Swami Amar Jyoti

If you had a choice you would never let go of the illusion.

> Ram Tzu

With courage you will dare to take risks, have the strength to be compassionate and the wisdom to be humble. Courage is the foundation of integrity.

> Keshavan Nair

Take someone who doesn't keep score, who's not looking to be richer, or afraid of losing, who has not the slightest interest even in his own personality: He's free.

> Rumi

God gives every bird its food, but He does not throw it into its nest.

> Buddhist Proverb

Asian Words of Inspiration

It is the clinging to the false that makes the true so difficult to see. Once you understand that the false needs time and what needs time is false, you are nearer the Reality, which is timeless, ever in the now. Eternity in time is mere repetitiveness, like the movement of a clock. It flows from the past into the future endlessly, as empty perpetuity. Reality is what makes the present so vital, so different from the past and future, which are merely mental. If you need time to achieve something, it must be false. The real is always with you; you need not wait to be what you are. Only you must not allow your mind to go out of yourself in search. When you want something, ask yourself: do I really need it? If the answer is not, then just drop it.

Nisargadatta Maharaj

What you need will come to you, if you do not ask for what you do not need. Yet only few people reach this state of complete dispassion and detachment. It is a very high state, the very threshold of liberation.

Nisargadatta Maharaj

If you do not change direction, you may end up where you are heading.

Lao-Tzu

Asian Words of Inspiration

The greatest guru is helpless as long as the disciple is not eager to learn. Eagerness and earnestness are all-important. Confidence will come with experience. Be devoted to your goal and devotion to him who can guide you will follow. If your desire and confidence are strong, they will operate and take you to your goal, for you will not cause delay by hesitation and compromise.

Nisargadatta Maharaj

Before embarking on important undertakings sit quietly, calm your senses and thoughts, and meditate deeply. You will then by guided by the creative power of Spirit. After that you should utilize all necessary means to achieve your goal.

Paramahansa Yogananda

Use only that which works and take it from any place you can find it.

Bruce Lee

If we are facing in the right direction, all we have to do is keep on walking.

Zen Proverb

Open your arms to change, but don't let go of your values.

Dalai Lama

Asian Words of Inspiration

All compromise is based on give and take, but there can be no give and take on fundamentals. Any compromise on fundamentals is a surrender.

Mohandas Karamchand (Mahatma) Gandhi

A superior man is modest in his speech, but exceeds in his actions.

Confucius

The way is not in the sky. The way is in the heart.

Buddha

Wherever you go, go with all your heart.

Confucius

Beginning is easy. Continuing is hard.

Japanese Proverb

No matter where you go – there you are.

Confucius

You have the infinite capacity to do anything you want. You compare yourself to others — that's why you feel so limited.

Kensho Furuya
Aikido master

Asian Words of Inspiration

You must be the change you want to see in the world.

> Mohandas Karamchand (Mahatma) Gandhi

The journey of a thousand miles must begin with a single step.

> Chinese Proverb

The various religions are like different roads converging on the same point. What difference does it make if we follow different routes, provided we arrive at the same destination?

> Mohandas Karamchand (Mahatma) Gandhi

If you can't bear the bite of a flea, how will you endure the bite of a snake? In appearance I am ruining your work, but in reality I am making a thorn into a rose garden.

> Rumi

When you do things from your soul, you feel a river moving in you, a joy.

> Rumi

There are two mistakes one can make along the road to truth: not going all the way and not starting.

> Buddha

Asian Words of Inspiration

A friend is one who does not disturb your mind. Maintain no friendship with ones who disturb your mind, no matter how close they are, be it a person, a place, or idea. Do not accept the invitations of foolish persons because when you live in their society truth will not kiss you.

Hariwansh Lal (Papaji) Poonja

A powerful interest which dominates a man's life polarizes his mind, which then acts like a magnet and continually draws out from his stored-up experience and also from new experiences whatever is relevant and useful to the end in view. Deep interest invigorates the mind, awakens its dormant powers and is the key to super excellence, invention, and discovery.

Swami Krishnananda Saraswati

It does not matter how slowly you go so long as you do not stop.

Confucius

You can't cross the sea merely by standing and staring at the water.

Rabindranath Tagore

Asian Words of Inspiration

The things you need in life are those that will help you to fulfill your dominant purpose. Things you may want but not need may lead you aside from that purpose. It is only by making everything serve your main objective that success is attained.

Paramahansa Yogananda

All power is within you. You can do anything and everything. Believe in that. Do not believe that you are weak; do not believe that you are half-crazy lunatics, as most of us do nowadays. Stand up and express the divinity within you.

Swami Vivekananda

The desire to find the self will surely be fulfilled, provided you want nothing else. But you must be honest with yourself and really want nothing else. If in the meantime you want many other things and are engaged in their pursuit, your main purpose may be delayed until you grow wiser and cease being torn between contradictory urges. Go within, without swerving, without ever looking outward.

Nisargadatta Maharaj

Action to be effective must be directed to clearly conceived ends.

Jawaharlal Nehru

Asian Words of Inspiration

It is impossible to organize things if you yourself are not in order. When you do things in the right way, at the right time, everything else will be organized.

Shunryu Suzuki

When you reach the top, keep climbing.

Zen Proverb

A doubt arises and is cleared. Another arises and that is cleared, making way for yet another; and so it goes on. So there is no possibility of clearing away all doubts. See to whom the doubts arise. Go to their source and abide in it. Then they cease to arise. That is how doubts are to be cleared.

Sri Ramana Maharshi

All that we are is the result of what we have thought. If a man speaks or acts with an evil thought, pain follows him. If a man speaks or acts with a pure thought, happiness follows him, like a shadow that never leaves him.

Buddha

The young do not know enough to be prudent, and therefore they attempt the impossible — and achieve it, generation after generation.

Pearl S. Buck

Asian Words of Inspiration

Man's attitude is the secret of life, for it is upon man's attitude that success and failure depend. Both man's rise and fall depend upon his attitude.

Inayat Khan

The higher your aims and vaster your desires, the more energy you will have for their fulfillment. Desire the good of all and the universe will work with you. But if you want your own pleasure, you must earn it the hard way. Before desiring, deserve.

Nisargadatta Maharaj

If you correct your mind, the rest of your life will fall into place.

Lao-Tzu

There are hundreds of paths up the mountain, all leading to the same place, so it doesn't matter which path you take. The only person wasting time is the one who runs around the mountain, telling everyone that his or her path is wrong.

Hindu Proverb

Asian Words of Inspiration

Those who have high thoughts are ever striving; they are not happy to remain in the same place.

> Buddha

Weak desires can be removed by introspection and meditation, but strong, deep-rooted ones must be fulfilled and their fruits, sweet or bitter, tasted.

> Nisargadatta Maharaj

Very often the answer to one's wishes is within one's reach, the hand of Providence not very far off, and then one loses one's patience and thereby the opportunity.

> Inayat Khan

Effort is necessary up to the state of realization. Even then the Self should spontaneously become evident, otherwise happiness will not be complete. Up to that state of spontaneity there must be effort in some form or another. There is a state beyond our efforts or effortlessness. Until it is realized effort is necessary. After tasting such bliss, even once, one will repeatedly try to regain it. Having once experienced the bliss of peace no one wants to be out of it or to engage in any other activity.

> Sri Ramana Maharshi

Asian Words of Inspiration

Human beings always cling to things. Practice begins when you stop clinging.

              Awa Kenzo

Manliness consists not in bluff, bravado, or lordliness. It consists in daring to do right and facing consequences, whether it is in matters social, political, or otherwise. It consists in deeds, not in words.

      Mohandas Karamchand (Mahatma) Gandhi

Retire when the work is done.

              Lao-Tzu

You may think your actions are meaningless and that they won't help, but that is no excuse. You must still act.

      Mohandas Karamchand (Mahatma) Gandhi

If you correct your mind, the rest of your life will fall into place.

              Lao-Tzu

You must find the place inside yourself where nothing is impossible.

             Deepak Chopra

Asian Words of Inspiration

The more man meditates upon good thoughts, the better will be his world and the world at large.

Confucius

The greatest carver does the least cutting.

Lao-Tzu

There is no best path or worst path. There is just the path to which each individual gets directed.

Ramesh S. Balsekar

Happiness comes when your work and words are of benefit to yourself and others.

Buddha

If you lose today, win tomorrow. In this never-ending spirit of challenge is the heart of a victor.

Daisaku Ikeda

Doing nothing is better than being busy doing nothing.

Lao-Tzu

Achieving your vision doesn't mean you've reached the end of the line. It simply means that you've come to a new starting place.

Nido Qubein

Asian Words of Inspiration

Do not undervalue attention. It means interest and also love. To know, to do, to discover, or to create you must give your heart to it — which means attention. All the blessings flow from it.

Nisargadatta Maharaj

The mind that perceives the limitation is the limitation.

Buddha

Know well what leads you forward and what holds you back, and choose the path that leads to wisdom.

Buddha

See the positive side, the potential. And make an effort.

Dalai Lama

By accepting life's goodness and offering it to benefit others, you will create true abundance in your own life.

Deepak Chopra

Take up one idea. Make that one idea your life — think of it, dream of it, live on that idea. Let the brain, muscles, nerves, every part of your body, be full of that idea, and just leave every other idea alone. This is the way to success, that is way great spiritual giants are produced.

Swami Vivekananda

Asian Words of Inspiration

One moment of patience may ward off great disaster. One moment of impatience may ruin a whole life.

Chinese Proverb

Absorb what is useful. Discard what is not. Add what is uniquely your own.

Bruce Lee

It is not so much what you believe in that matters, as the way in which you believe it and proceed to translate that belief into action.

Lin Yutang

The superior man acts before he speaks, and afterward speaks according to his action.

Confucius

The person who runs away exposes himself to that very danger more than a person who sits quietly.

Jawaharlal Nehru

Acquire a firm will and the utmost patience.

Sri Anandamayi Ma

Fashion your life as a garland of beautiful deeds.

Buddha

Asian Words of Inspiration

Yield and overcome; bend and be straight; empty and be full; Wear out and be new; have little and gain; have much and be confused. Therefore wise men embrace the one and set an example to all. Not putting on a display, they shine forth. Not justifying themselves, they are distinguished. Not boasting, they receive recognition. Not bragging, they never falter. They do not quarrel, so no one quarrels with them. Therefore the ancients say "Yield and overcome." Is that an empty saying? Be really whole and all things will come to you.

Lao-Tzu

Put your heart, mind, intellect, and soul even to your smallest acts. This is the secret of success.

Swami Sivananda

Asian Words of Inspiration

Interconnectedness

The most interesting thing about a photo of earth taken from space is that there are no borders or geographic divisions. It's one planet. With one people.

Or, as Sufi poet Rumi wrote, *"There is one being in all of us."*

When you pause to consider that there are over seven billion souls running around this planet, being concerned about other people is not just a question of humanity — it becomes the foundation of spirituality. For when you think of these seven billion people as souls, instead of seeing them as human beings, an immediate sense of interconnectedness arises.

Focus on the interconnectedness of our spirits, the differences in our human characteristics no longer matter. Nor do the man-made divisions of borders and cultural divides.

As spiritual beings occupying temporary vessels of the human form, we are connected to the whole of humanity on three distinct levels: human, spiritual, and eternal.

Asian Words of Inspiration

Unfortunately, too many of us neither see this nor understand it.

Which is why Thich Nhat Hanh advises, *"We are here to awaken from the illusion of separateness."*

In this section you will find the thoughts of other leading Asian thinkers on the interconnectedness of life and spirituality.

The reason why the universe is eternal is that it does not live for itself; it gives life to others as it transforms.

Lao-Tzu

Bigotry tries to keep truth safe in its hand with a grip that kills it.

Rabindranath Tagore

Inherent in every intention and desire is the mechanics for its fulfillment....intention and desire in the field of pure potentiality have infinite organizing power.

Deepak Chopra

Asian Words of Inspiration

Come out into the broad light of day, come out from the little narrow paths, for how can the infinite soul rest content to live and die in small ruts? Come out into the universe of Light. Everything in the universe is yours, stretch out your arms and embrace it with love. If you ever felt you wanted to do that, you have felt God.

Swami Vivekananda

In reality only the Ultimate is. The rest is a matter of name and form. And as long as you cling to the idea that only what has name and shape exists, the Supreme will appear to you as non-existing. When you understand that names and shapes are hollow shells without any content whatsoever, and what is real is nameless and formless, pure energy of life and light of consciousness, you will be at peace — immersed in the deep silence of reality.

Nisargadatta Maharaj

In our willingness to step into the unknown, the field of all possibilities, we surrender ourselves to the creative mind that orchestrates the dance of the universe.

Deepak Chopra

Asian Words of Inspiration

For a better, happier, more stable and civilized future, each of us must develop a sincere, warm-hearted feeling of brother and sisterhood.

Dalai Lama

If you want to awaken all of humanity, then awaken all of yourself, if you want to eliminate the suffering in the world, then eliminate all that is dark and negative in yourself. Truly, the greatest gift you have to give is that of your own self-transformation.

Lao-Tzu

The whole universe exists in the spirit, by the spirit, for the spirit; all we do, think, and feel is for the spirit.

Sri Aurobindo

When you are writing, is it the nib writing? The eyes are unable to see what is behind the visible form. Hence the sense of isolation of activities. When the little finger moves, the child thinks that only the little finger is moving. But mature minds with knowledge of the working of the human body know that the whole physiology of the human system is behind the movement of the little finger.

Swami Krishnananda Saraswati

Asian Words of Inspiration

No sound of clapping comes from only one hand. The thirsty man is moaning "O delicious water!" The water is calling "Where is the one who will drink me?" This thirst in our souls is the magnetism of the water: We are its, and it is ours.

Rumi

At the phenomenal level the only thing that is not a concept is this knowledge which every single human being, every single sentient being at every time in history, has known: I exist, I am in this moment, here and now.

Ramesh S. Balsekar

I believe in the law of cause and effect. I just doesn't know which is which.

Ram Tzu

It's sheer illusion to try to separate the phenomena from the Reality, and then try to love phenomena first. It just doesn't happen that way. Naturally we end in failure. You don't have to try to achieve unity with others. It is fallacious thinking and doing. Realize the unity of everything and everyone within you first.

Swami Amar Jyoti

Asian Words of Inspiration

Wisdom is not negation of anything. Everything is okay from His point of view. That is why God does not interfere with anything. Everything is okay for Him, because every point of view is His point of view.

Swami Krishnananda Saraswati

You indulge in Self Improvement and all you have to show for it is an improved self.

Ram Tzu

To me you are your own God. But if you think otherwise, think to the end. If there be God, then all is God's and all is for the best. Welcome all that comes with a glad and thankful heart. And love all creatures. This too will take you to your Self.

Nisargadatta Maharaj

Individually, we are one drop. Together, we are an ocean.

Ryunosuke Satoro

Everything happens altogether by itself. The shadow of causation can never be caught because all things and events are merely interconnected differentiations in form of a single, unified field.

Ramesh S. Balsekar

Asian Words of Inspiration

When you know beyond all doubting that the same life flows through all that is and you are that life, you will love all naturally and spontaneously. When you realize the depth and fullness of your love of yourself, you know that every living being and the entire universe are included in your affection.

                                          Nisargadatta Maharaj

We are here to awaken from the illusion of our separateness.

                                          Thich Nhat Hanh

The heart of a human being is no different from the soul of heaven and earth. In your practices always keep in your thoughts the interaction of heaven and earth, water and fire, yin and yang.

                                          Morihei Ueshiba

Interdependence is and ought to be as much the ideal of man as self-sufficiency. Man is a social being.

                              Mohandas Karamchand (Mahatma) Gandhi

Just as one's dream in sleep exists nowhere but in the mind (both as cause and effect) so does the universe exist only in the mind of infinite Consciousness.

                                        Ramesh S. Balsekar

Asian Words of Inspiration

If you can be independent of the world, then you can see God in everything. The difference of opposites is the obstacle that prevents you from seeing God in everything, because the opposites do not exist in God; they cease to be opposites in God. God is positive in its entirety.

                         Swami Krishnananda Saraswati

There is no chaos in the world, except the chaos which your mind creates. It is self-created in the sense that at its very center is the false idea of oneself as a thing different and separate from other things. In reality you are not a thing, nor separate. You are the infinite potentiality, the inexhaustible possibility. Because you are, all can be. The universe is but a partial manifestation of your limitless capacity to become.

                                   Nisargadatta Maharaj

Anything you do for the sake of enlightenment takes you nearer. Anything you do without remembering enlightenment puts you off. But why complicate? Just know that you are above and beyond all things and thoughts. What you want to be, you are it already. Just keep it in mind.

                                   Nisargadatta Maharaj

Asian Words of Inspiration

It's not the Cosmos that's going to tumble down back into your bottleneck, into the bottle; it's the breath in the bottle which has to mingle with the Cosmic breath. It's the Oneness which the objective world has to seek rather than expecting the subjective Divine to descend into egotistical bottles with labels on them.

Swami Amar Jyoti

What you are seeking is seeking you.

Rumi

Empty your mind of all thoughts. Let your heart be at peace. Watch the turmoil of beings, but contemplate their return. Each separate being in the Universe returns to the common source. Returning to the source is serenity.

Lao-Tzu

From the beginning nothing is. There really has never been any beginning, nor is there any end. The universe is a dream. So is the one who is supposed to understand this! Belief in oneself is, in fact, the only real obstruction to awakening from delusion.

Ramesh S. Balsekar

Asian Words of Inspiration

All conundrums, all apparent riddles, paradoxes and contradictions subsist only in the split-mind based on subject-object relationship. They resolve themselves as soon as they are seen from the viewpoint of Totality.

Ramesh S. Balsekar

Which God are you talking about? What is God? Is he not the very light by which you ask the question? "I am" itself is God. The seeking itself is God. In seeking you discover that you are neither the body nor mind, and the love of self in you is for the self in all. The two are one. The consciousness in you and the consciousness in me, apparently two, really one, seek unity and that is love.

Nisargadatta Maharaj

The ocean itself is one big drop, but it is also made of small drops; many little drops put together become an ocean. But actually, in the ocean, the drops don't exist; they are one integral whole. So, you may say there are no drops in the ocean, yet you can say it is made up of drops. Both notions are correct. Actually, the drops in the ocean are only conceptual. The mind says that there are many parts. Ideas move the world.

Swami Krishnananda Saraswati

Asian Words of Inspiration

Nature never does a bad thing. There is no such thing as a bad thing for Nature. It looks unpleasant, because we are outside nature, psychologically. If we are one with Nature, we will see nothing improper taking place. We are looking at things by standing outside nature. That is why we cannot see things properly and impartially.

Swami Krishnananda Saraswati

Without self-realization no virtue is genuine. It is only when you arrive at the deepest conviction that the same life flows through everything, and that you ARE that life, that you can begin to love naturally and spontaneously.

Ramesh S. Balsekar

Only that which was prior to the appearance of this body-consciousness is your true identity. That is Reality. It is here and now, and there is no question of anyone being able to reach for it or grasp it.

Ramesh S. Balsekar

The nature of Consciousness is such that it simultaneously pervades the past, present, and future and can experience infinite varieties of universes. But all is merely the play of Consciousness itself.

Ramesh S. Balsekar

Asian Words of Inspiration

Interdependence is a fundamental law of nature. Even tiny insects survive by cooperating with each other. Our own survival is so dependent on the help of others that a need for love lies at the very core of our existence. This is why we need to cultivate a genuine sense of responsibility and a sincere concern for the welfare of others.

Dalai Lama

About the Author

**Steven Howard
Global Leadership Development and Facilitation
Leadership Coach | Keynote Speaker**

Steven Howard specializes in creating and delivering Leadership Development curriculum for frontline leaders, mid-level leaders, senior leaders and high-potential leaders.

An author with 36 years of international senior sales, marketing, and leadership experience, his corporate career covered a wide variety of fields and experiences, including Regional Marketing Director for Texas Instruments Asia-Pacific, South Asia & ASEAN Regional Director for TIME Magazine, Global Account Director at BBDO Advertising handling an international airline account, and VP Marketing for Citibank's Consumer Banking Group.

Since 1988 he has delivered leadership development training programs in the U.S., Asia, Australia, Africa, Canada and Europe to numerous organizations, including Citicorp, Covidien, DBS Bank, Deutsche Bank, DuPont Lycra, Esso Productions, ExxonMobil, Hewlett Packard Enterprise,

Asian Words of Inspiration

Micron Technology, Motorola Solutions, SapientNitro, Standard Chartered Bank, and many others.

He has been a member of the training faculty at MasterCard University Asia/Pacific, the Citibank Asia-Pacific Banking Institute, and Forum Corporation. He brings a truly international, cross-cultural perspective to his leadership development programs, having lived in the USA for 26 years, in Singapore for 21 years and in Australia for 12 years.

In addition to his leadership facilitation work Steven has served on several Boards in both the private and non-profit sectors. He has also chaired a strategic advisory group for a local government entity and a national sporting organization that is a member of the Australian Olympic Committee.

Steven is the author of 16 marketing, management, and leadership books and is the editor of three professional and personal development books in the *Project You* series.

His books are:

Corporate Image Management: *A Marketing Discipline*

Powerful Marketing Minutes: *50 Ways to Develop Market Leadership*

MORE Powerful Marketing Minutes: *50 New Ways to Develop Market Leadership*

Asian Words of Inspiration

Asian Words of Wisdom

Asian Words of Knowledge

Essential Asian Words of Wisdom

Pillars of Growth: *Strategies for Leading Sustainable Growth* (co-author with three others)

Motivation Plus Marketing Equals Money (co-author with four others)

Marketing Words of Wisdom

The Best of the Monday Morning Marketing Memo

Powerful Marketing Memos

8 Keys To Becoming A Great Leader (With Leadership Lessons and Tips from Gibbs, Yoda and Capt'n Jack Sparrow)

Asian Words of Success

Asian Words of Meaning

Asian Words of Inspiration

The Book of Asian Proverbs

www.ingramcontent.com/pod-product-compliance
Lightning Source LLC
Chambersburg PA
CBHW061323040426
42444CB00011B/2742